Live Online Learning

Palgrave Teaching and Learning

Series Editor: **Sally Brown**

Facilitating Workshops
For the Love of Learning
Leading Dynamic Seminars
Live Online Learning

Further titles are in preparation

Universities into the 21st Century

Series Editors: **Noel Entwistle and Roger King**

Becoming an Academic
Cultures and Change in Higher Education
Global Inequalities in Higher Education
Learning Development in Higher Education
Managing Your Academic Career
Managing Your Career in Higher Education Administration
Research and Teaching
Teaching Academic Writing in UK Higher Education
Teaching for Understanding at University
Understanding the International Student Experience
The University in the Global Age
Writing in the Disciplines

Palgrave Research Skills

Authoring a PhD
The Foundations of Research (2nd edn)
Getting to Grips with Doctoral Research
The Good Supervisor (2nd edn)
Maximizing the Impacts of University Research
The Postgraduate Research Handbook (2nd edn)
The Professional Doctorate
Structuring Your Research Thesis

You may also be interested in:

Teaching Study Skills and Supporting Learning

For a complete listing of all our titles in this area please visit
www.palgrave.com/studyskills

Live Online Learning

Strategies for the Web Conferencing Classroom

Sarah Cornelius
Carole Gordon
Jan Schyma

palgrave
macmillan

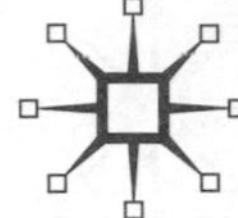

First published 2014 by
PALGRAVE MACMILLAN

Palgrave Macmillan in the UK is an imprint of Macmillan Publishers Limited, registered in England, company number 785998, of Houndmills, Basingstoke, Hampshire RG21 6XS.

Palgrave Macmillan in the US is a division of St Martin's Press LLC, 175 Fifth Avenue, New York, NY 10010.

Palgrave Macmillan is the global academic imprint of the above companies and has companies and representatives throughout the world.

Palgrave® and Macmillan® are registered trademarks in the United States, the United Kingdom, Europe and other countries

ISBN: 978–1–137–32875–5

This book is printed on paper suitable for recycling and made from fully managed and sustained forest sources. Logging, pulping and manufacturing processes are expected to conform to the environmental regulations of the country of origin.

A catalogue record for this book is available from the British Library.

A catalog record for this book is available from the Library of Congress.

Typeset by Cambrian Typesetters, Camberley, Surrey

Printed in China

Contents

List of figures and tables

Figures

Tables

Preface

Live online learning is learning in real time in a virtual classroom using web conferencing software. It creates opportunities for participants in different locations to get together and share learning experiences using a range of multimedia technologies. There is a common perception that web conferencing offers little more than a facilitated meeting space: in fact it offers much more. This book aims to show how live online learning can provide opportunities for highly visual, fast-paced collaborative activities which enhance learning.

Live online learning is increasingly used in teaching and training. Universities, colleges and businesses have developed courses which depend on web conferencing, and facilitators need support and resources to make this environment a success. This book is for new and experienced tutors and trainers in universities, colleges and business, those undertaking professional teaching qualifications, learning technologists and staff development personnel. Experiences of learners and facilitators are brought together to provide practical support for those new to this environment and for those wanting to develop creative and innovative practice.

The opening chapter aims to inspire you with some examples of the possibilities that web conferencing provides for teaching and learning. Those that follow take you on a journey from the initial preparations necessary for live online learning, through to the assessment of learning online and beyond.

The book is written to be independent of any particular software product, and we do not go into great depth on technical issues. To participate in live online learning you need to have access to appropriate hardware and the internet, but requirements are generally minimal, with a robust internet connection and good quality audio tools being key to success. There is a wide range of software products you can use, including some that have been designed with the needs of teaching and learning in mind. Our experience has been with a variety of tools, including Elluminate Live!, Collaborate, Adobe Connect and Google Hangouts, but there are many others available, some very expensive, and others freely available online. The focus in this book is on teaching and learning issues, so there is no attempt to review or evaluate different products. We concentrate on how to use the software effectively and creatively to provide engaging learning opportunities. As a result, you may find it helpful to read the book alongside software manuals and guidelines relevant to the products you have available in your own context.

The idea of student centred learning underpins our practice as educators in Further, Higher and Professional education, and throughout the book we put learners first. We strongly believe that learners' needs and characteristics should influence the decisions that teachers and trainers make when designing and facilitating live online learning. Learners' experiences and stories are therefore used throughout the book, and will be particularly helpful for facilitators who have limited experience themselves as learners in virtual classrooms. Tutors' experiences are also an important part of the text. Some of the real experiences, presented as case studies, are based on the authors' practice. Others were collected during reflective team discussions, and some were obtained during discussions and interviews with colleagues and learners. We have tried to stay as close to the original words used as possible, but some editing has been necessary to fit the style of the book and to maintain anonymity. The tutor stories are all real experiences, and learner stories are inspired by and recreated from genuine situations. Some changes have been made to the original scenarios to ensure that individual learners are not identifiable.

The formal research underpinning this book was carried out by the authors over a three year period, including a project funded by ELESIG (elesig.ning.com) and research supported by the University of Aberdeen. These projects aimed to help us gain a better understanding of teachers' and learners' experiences in virtual classrooms and support the development of engaging and effective learning activities. Full details of the work undertaken can be found in Cornelius and Gordon (2012 and 2013) and Cornelius (2013a and 2013b). The findings from these projects have informed staff development activities delivered within and beyond the University of Aberdeen, and discussions with colleagues from a range of institutions have helped to deepen our understanding of experiences of live online learning.

A selection of recommended books and other sources of further reading is included at the end of the book. There is, to date, a relatively small body of easily accessible research and advice specifically on live online learning, so the suggestions include books from the wider literature on online learning, and on teaching and learning in Further and Higher education.

We have been inspired to write this book because we have enjoyed the challenge of providing effective live online learning for participants. Our own experiences in a range of settings in universities and colleges, our own research, and the experiences of many other facilitators and evidence from published research have also helped to shape the insights, strategies and resources presented. We hope this book will help you succeed as a live online facilitator.

Acknowledgements

Writing this book has been a team effort and we would like to thank everyone who has contributed. Our biggest thank you goes to Lorna Johnson, who led us into the virtual classroom and shared the writing journey with us. Our colleagues Yvonne Bain and Chris Aldred also shared our experience of learning to be online tutors and we are very grateful to them for their contributions.

Many others have contributed to the book in different ways. A big thank you is due to Suzie Clement who prepared the diagrams and illustrations. Colleagues from the University of Aberdeen and beyond have shared their experiences of web conferencing and supported our research activities and the writing of this book. We are very grateful for all their help and support. We would also like to thank our online students who shared our learning experience and gave us so much valuable feedback.

Many thanks are due to Jennifer Schmidt, Della Oliver and Suzannah Burywood and the team at Palgrave Macmillan for all their support. Finally, we would like to thank Gail MacLeod and Lynda Cooper who introduced us to Palgrave.

Series editor's preface

This new series of books with Palgrave, for all who care about teaching and learning in higher education, is launched with the express aim of providing useful, relevant, current and helpful guidance on key issues in learning and teaching in the tertiary/post-compulsory education sector. This is currently an area of very rapid and unpredictable change, with universities and colleges reviewing and often implementing radical alterations in the ways they design, deliver and assess the curriculum, taking into account not just innovations in the way that content is being delivered and supported, particularly through technological means, but also the changing relationships between academics and their students. The role of the teacher in higher education needs to be reconsidered when students can freely access content worldwide and seek accreditation and recognition of learning by local, national or international providers (and may indeed prefer to do so). Students internationally are becoming progressively more liable for the payment of fees, as higher education becomes seen as less of a public good and more of a private one, and this, too, changes the nature of the transaction.

Texts in this series will address these and other emergent imperatives. Among topics covered will be student centred approaches at undergraduate and postgraduate levels including doctoral work, the necessity to work in an internationalised and transnational tertiary education context, the challenges of staff–student interactions where engagements are as likely to be through new technologies as face to face in the classroom, and issues about the levels of student engagement, especially where study is in competition with other demands on their time, including employment and caring responsibilities. This text on live online learning provides a welcome contribution to the series.

Sally Brown
September 2013

Series editor's preface

1 Be inspired ...

... to learn more about the experience of teaching and learning in a web conferencing environment.

This chapter introduces you to:

- the virtual classroom
- ways of creating a learning space in a meeting place
- inspiring learners
- inspiring facilitators
- the learner centred teaching approach
- the issues, strategies and resources explored in this book.

The virtual classroom

Welcome to a virtual classroom.

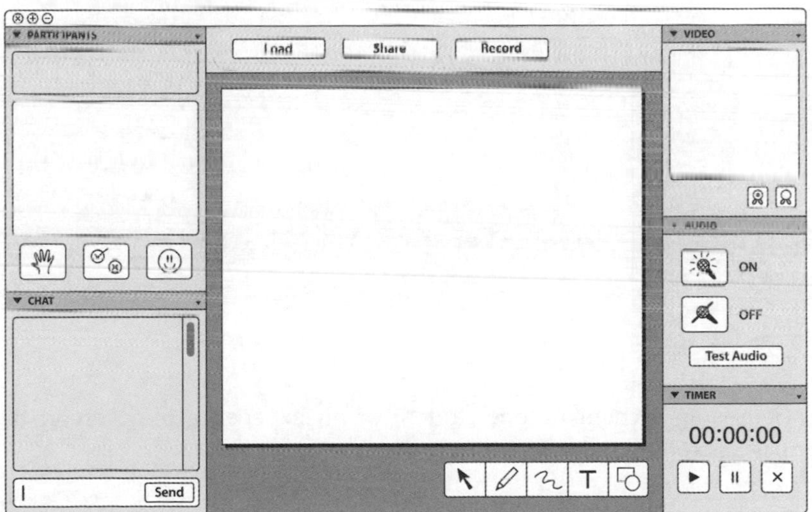

Figure 1.1 The empty classroom

Like most empty classrooms this is not very inspiring! The aim of this book is to reveal the potential of this empty screen to become an exciting learning space.

The virtual classroom is created using web conferencing technology, which allows participants in different locations to get together and share learning experiences, using a wide range of multimedia learning resources. Web conferencing is well known as a resource for business meetings, but it also offers opportunities for highly visual, interactive learning experiences.

Web conferencing technology varies depending on the supplier and is constantly being updated and developed. However, there are key components in the technology which replicate the physical spaces and resources that we use at work and in education. Most importantly, there is a room where people can meet. This is a web location and participants are given a link which allows them to access the virtual classroom. Most participants then see something like the screen in Figure 1.2.

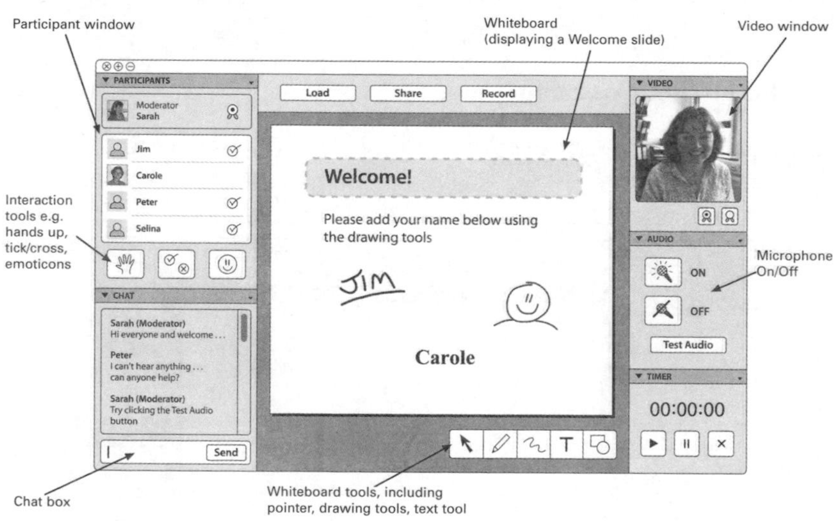

Figure 1.2 The virtual classroom

Here is an account by one student of his experience of accessing the virtual classroom for the first time.

My tutor sent me a link to the classroom and access was quick and easy. I arrived in the room, not entirely sure what I'd find. There was a list of participants on the left and my name was there with about four other people who had already signed in. Some had photos beside their names. I was really pleased when the tutor showed us how to add a photo for ourselves. (I'm not a fan of my own photo but it was so much better to see a face rather than an outline beside my name.) I was impressed that I was able to do this task so easily too. I'd been told in the welcome email to do an audio test when I arrived. Again this was simple and when I'd finished the tutor greeted me and told me how to switch on the microphone so that I could reply. Others in the group had posted messages in the chat box, some expressing worries about the technology and others offering reassurance, all very friendly. There was a welcome slide on the screen and the tutor had created a space for us to sign our names. I was slow to get the hang of the pen tool and only managed a childlike signature but everyone else was the same and someone added a smiley face which helped to lighten the moment. When the whole group had signed in, the tutor asked us to use the tick symbol to let her know that we were ready to start. I was definitely ready to go – and very surprised at how easy and motivating it all seemed.

This example refers to many of the tools that are common in web conferencing systems. Participants in the virtual classroom can talk to one another using a microphone, and see one another using a web cam. Many students would expect to receive notes or handouts during a lesson. These can be provided online through a file sharing system. All the materials used in an online session can be saved, including the commentary in the chat box. Additional 'rooms' can be created for group work. Instructions on the main screen can be sent to these breakout rooms, and ideas generated by small groups in the breakout rooms can be sent back to the main room for everyone to see.

Our experience of working with web conferencing systems suggests that many of the things that can be done in physical educational settings are possible online. Perhaps the most exciting discovery is that it is possible to do some things in the virtual classroom that are more difficult in a face to face situation. An online tutor provided the following commentary on the experience of working in a virtual classroom.

There is an efficiency about the virtual classroom which I find very pleasing as a tutor. The almost instantaneous movement of participants into breakout rooms is wonderful, in comparison to moving chairs in a normal classroom and then trying to create enough space for each group to be heard without shouting. In the main room everyone can see the screen and students can annotate the screen without having to leave their seats. There are also fewer distractions in the virtual classroom and this can increase the focus on learning. Students have to indicate that they want to speak using the hands up tool, and this also seems to lead to more relevant interaction. Even applause is efficient as they all press a button and clapping signs appear beside their names!

The experience of discovering the potential of the virtual classroom described in this example is increasingly common. Universities, colleges and businesses have developed courses which depend on web conferencing, and facilitators need support and resources to make this environment a success. Perhaps that is why you are reading this book and want to know more about creating learning spaces online.

Creating a learning space in a meeting place

Web conferencing systems are designed to allow people in different locations to come together online and talk to one another. This is an invaluable resource for business, helping to reduce the time and cost involved in travelling to meetings. Educationalists and students have also embraced the efficiency of meeting online, but are very aware that learning is about more than just talking. The challenge of using web conferencing to create a virtual classroom has provided insights into the teaching and learning process and informed debate about how learners can use new technology to access learning in ways not imagined before.

Web conferencing allows learners to share their learning experience with other students and their tutor. The synchronous, or real time, nature of online learning through web conferencing creates a very specific opportunity for those involved – to engage with one another and to share the learning experience. If the tutor or trainer uses the facility merely to deliver a presentation and ignores all the interactive resources this opportunity is lost: a video would have been just as useful. Live online learning is a two way process and getting feedback from students is very easy. This allows tutors and trainers to know something about what participants are thinking, feeling and learning. One way communication can be achieved very effectively using a video or podcast. Web conferencing is different and has the potential to do much more. Already in this introduction we have mentioned a wide range of different tools that are available in the virtual classroom. Although many of these tools are available elsewhere, perhaps what is special about web conferencing is the combination of these tools, the ease of access, and the diversity of media in one package.

This book focuses specifically on applications of web conferencing in a teaching and learning context, permitting interaction between teachers and learners, between learners and other learners, and between learners and resources. In an educational context the tools available allow us to provide opportunities for learning which build on many of the principles of learning that we know are most likely to work. These include the use of media and teaching approaches which meet learner needs and preferences, including discussion and collaboration. Research undertaken in higher education and school contexts across the globe has demonstrated that learners view live online learning favourably (McBrien and Jones, 2009; Ward, Peters and Shelley, 2010). They benefit from opportunities for interaction and demonstrate improved outcomes when they interact online with other learners in real time. However, researchers have also emphasised that using appropriate pedagogical approaches is important (De Freitas and Neumann, 2009; Murphy, Rodríguez-Manzanares and Barbour, 2010). It is essential to use the online tools to enhance the learning experience, not merely because they are available. Technology can be very clever and very entertaining, but can also distract learners if used inappropriately, and it can limit their engagement with the learning experience.

In this book, there will be many examples of how this engagement can be achieved in a virtual classroom. Here is an example from someone who had used web conferencing as a meeting place but was 'blown away' by her experience of it as a learning space. This tutor attended an event for colleagues interested in using web conferencing in their teaching. Participants were invited to log on from their offices. The basics of an online learning session were demonstrated, showing the tools that can be used and how to make a session truly participative. Participants were invited to work together in simple group tasks.

> We've been using web conferencing for meetings and tutorials for some time. The interactive whiteboard is also commonly used in our organisation. My reservation about both of these technologies was that they use lots of slides and information on screen, with commentary from the presenter. There was often an element of 'death by PowerPoint' as presenters struggled to keep our interest. When there was discussion in our team about using web conferencing for training purposes, my heart sank as I imagined the modern version of chalk and talk! However, when I first saw web conferencing used for training I was blown away by the creative use

of the space and the high level of interaction between participants and learners, and actually between learners and learners. Suddenly, I was able to see the potential of web conferencing. The session opened up possibilities that I hadn't thought of. I left with a determination to rethink the use of online teaching sessions with my own students.

The virtual classroom becomes the lively learning space that this tutor experienced because of the way it is used. Turning a meeting space into a learning space is about creating participative and interesting activities that will engage all learners in a live online group.

Inspiring learners

Learners online have also been inspired by the virtual classroom. Evidence from our research (Cornelius and Gordon, 2012) suggests that learners may be anxious when they first approach the virtual classroom, but soon gain confidence and an awareness of the benefits of live online learning. A learner describes this experience.

The most surprising thing was how focused I was on the topic. In an ordinary classroom my mind often wanders. I'm a people watcher and I look at other students or glance out of the window. Online I found it easier to concentrate. There was always something useful to look at on the whiteboard and the tutor was easy to listen to. She kept bringing us into the session or we could signal that we wanted to speak. There was a lot going on to keep my attention, including a chat box, breakout rooms and activities.

This student found the participative nature of live online learning and the lack of distractions helpful. In an interview about the experience of teaching online, one tutor commented on the quality of contributions from online learners.

The learning that took place during live online activities seemed to me to be of a very high quality, perhaps more so than in face to face classes. I would also say that some of the contributions we had from the student investigations were excellent. We had some fabulous presentations. The students had learned how to put slides on screen through application sharing, but they also included activities. They had to think about how to manage this online, in a way that they may not have thought about had they been in a normal classroom.

Another tutor commented on the potential for deeper and more meaningful dialogue online, and the students' apparent willingness to offer more of themselves than they might do in a normal classroom.

We asked all the students in the group to share a story about their experience of being an adult learner returning to education after being employed or bringing up a family. The stories were amazing and often inspirational. They talked about the difficulties they had experienced at school and the courage needed to come back to education. There were touching comments about the people who had believed in them and shocking comments about people who had mocked their ambition to return to education. Although we had experience of doing this kind of activity in the classroom with a face to face group, we had never experienced such openness as we experienced with the online group. It felt as if the lack of eye contact and nonverbal communication offered a unique opportunity for talking about personal experiences.

These positive accounts of inspiring learners give an insight into what is possible. Not all learners will find it easy to be open online or to present excellent work, but knowing what is possible may inspire facilitators to be bold in their expectations of learners.

Inspiring facilitators

The purpose of all the strategies described in this book is to promote the interactive approach that is available in live online learning. Research interviews with both new and experienced facilitators of online learning suggest that working in the virtual classroom has resulted in new insights into teaching and learning. These insights have been inspirational for the facilitators and led to greater awareness of learner needs. This is seen in the following examples given by two online tutors as they reflect on their experience of working in virtual classrooms.

I thought the challenges would be technological. I don't think I anticipated the pedagogical challenges. I think I was aware that teaching methods would have to be different, but I was hung up on the process of the technology, not on the way it would be used. It's been a real opportunity to learn about what I can do and what I can't do as a teacher. It's made me value some of the things that I can do in a way that I hadn't valued them before. There was also a touch of complacency about skills and strategies that I thought I could just transfer to another environment. It's been a really important professional learning opportunity.

I'm not sure that the differences between online and face to face teaching were as great as I thought they might be. The support that was provided for the participants who were working online was as good, if not better than the support that I would provide for participants working face to face. We did lose the opportunity for the sort of casual conversations that you have if you're in the face to face situation, where just as people are arriving you would chat and so you would know more about them personally. I think that participants were more focused online and this came through in the responses they gave, as if they had prepared what they wanted to say. Maybe because they couldn't see one another they wanted to make sure that any response was a valuable one. There were definitely things that were very positive about learning in an online environment.

Being a facilitator in any learning situation can be very challenging. There is the same need to get to know learners, to develop appropriate and interesting ways of involving them in the learning process, and also to be sure that their objectives in taking the course are met. Throughout this book, there are references to skills and behaviour that will be familiar to all tutors and trainers. Even when the environment changes, the principles and practice of teaching and learning are fundamentally about meeting learner needs. This is the philosophy which underpins this book.

▶ The learner centred teaching approach

The learner centred teaching approach is a philosophy which supports the decisions that tutors and trainers make in preparing and delivering education and training. Very simply, the learner centred teaching approach always directs us to learner needs and how they can be met in the context of the learning experience. This is an important ideological perspective for online learning. Decisions are not made because the technology has a particular tool that it would be fun to use, or software has been introduced that would impress our students. Decisions about learning online are made on the basis of what will help learners to be successful in their chosen course. Any limitations of online learning provide a challenge to the facilitator to be true to the learner centred teaching approach. Decisions about how to use the technology and the content of workshops and tutorials must be based on what will work for the students.

This comment from a tutor taking part in a focus group on online learning reflects on the importance of engaging learners online and illustrates the learner centred approach in action.

> For me, all of this is about engagement with the learner. What I find particularly reassuring is that the learners often set out with great apprehension and scepticism about doing things in the online environment, but very quickly those feelings are turned around. It becomes something that they enjoy doing and that they are happy to engage with. They realise that this is a good learning process. For me that says it all! If the learners feel that this environment helps them to engage in the learning process that's what matters. This engagement does depend on how you are using the technology. It has to be with really purposeful activities that are dynamic and engaging for learners and enable the learner to have a voice within the session as well.

Our research into learner preferences has been very helpful in determining the choices we make to meet learner needs. Some choices have been very simple. The use of the web cam for example, feels as if it will provide a more real and personal feel to any virtual classroom. This can be true at certain points in any course, but it is also possible that the facilitator will distract learners with apparently robotic movements and lack of eye contact when looking at the screen or notes, rather than at the camera. Similarly, if all the participants use web cams, there can be too many faces and movements that can catch the eye and distract attention from the learning experience. Our learners expressed a preference for the web cam to be switched on during the opening of a session and then switched off when learning activities were under way. It was important that the learners made this decision about how the online learning experience could be enhanced.

Our research also suggested that learners quickly get used to the technology and enjoy using it in interactive ways. If the facilitator misses opportunities for learners to take part in the learning process they can quickly lose interest, and over time forget how to use the range of tools in the system. This suggests that there are several levels of interaction for tutors and trainers to consider. On one level, information has to be presented, and skills and ways of thinking have to be developed. This is familiar territory. There is also a need to encourage interaction in an environment where it is possible to be almost invisible. This level involves careful planning so that interaction is a definite part of the learning process. An additional layer that is specific to the virtual classroom is to develop the technical skills of participants so that they are able to make the best use of the learning environment. The final example continues the story of the new learner who described his introduction to the virtual classroom at the beginning of this chapter.

> The workshop was quite fast paced with lots of changes of activity and lots of interaction. We were expected to do a lot! I was exhausted at the end of it! The tutor made use of what she called 'breakout' rooms. We had to 'drag' ourselves into our allocated room to meet in small groups. What we were dragging was actually our name from the participants' list, but I was very surprised to be able to move myself around the space in this way. We had small group activities to do, and anything we put on the whiteboard in our breakout room was then transferred to the main room. The technology was amazing, but in a supportive way. My main focus was still on the content and the activities, but I was aware that I was learning a lot about working in a virtual classroom as well as the course I'd enrolled for. It was hard to explain to my wife what it was like – her eyes were glazing over a bit – as I tried to get across to her what it looked like and how challenged and excited I felt.

The engagement with the technology and the learning experience described by this learner, suggests that the approach used by his tutor was truly learner centred. It is easy for tutors and trainers to lose sight of the learner because the technology makes so many demands on their attention. Later in the book an experienced tutor speaks of the way the online environment took her back to the early days of her teaching career. This was a time of being teacher centred, focusing on her delivery and what mattered to her, rather than being learner centred. Her view is that the technology disabled the learner centred skills that she had acquired as an experienced tutor and there was a need to relearn how to be learner centred.

Read on ...

This book is about teaching and learning in the web conferencing classroom. New learning environments can be just as intimidating for experienced tutors and trainers as for people who are new to the profession. This book is designed for anyone who is responsible for delivering live online learning, or for anyone who just wants to know more about how it works.

Our objectives are:

- to provide **insights** into the challenges and potential of live online learning
- to inspire readers to develop creative and innovative **strategies** for teaching and learning, building on best practice and research evidence
- to provide **suggestions for activities** that facilitators can use and adapt for their own learners.

Each chapter takes you through a different aspect of teaching and learning online, including case studies and examples to support practical information and theoretical perspectives. There are also suggestions that you can adapt for use in your own virtual classroom or as a starting point for developing inspiring learning activities.

IN SUMMARY

We hope that this chapter has inspired you to read on and develop your understanding of the creative potential of web conferencing for live online learning.

- **The virtual classroom** offers a powerful interactive tool to allow learners to meet online wherever they are situated. It simulates a normal classroom space and offers some additional opportunities for learners and facilitators.
- **Creating a learning space in a meeting place** is the main aim of the online facilitator. However useful the technology, without the creativity of the facilitator, web conferencing offers only a meeting place.
- **Inspiring learners** has a double meaning. Live online learning provides many examples of learners who inspire tutors and trainers to use the technology to create an even more powerful learning

tool. The virtual classroom can also inspire learners by opening up learning opportunities and collaborative working which adds a vital dimension to learning.

- **Inspiring facilitators** also has a double meaning. The purpose of this introduction was to inspire readers to find out more about the potential of the virtual classroom. It is also about the potential to be inspirational facilitators, developing creative and innovative learning approaches online.
- **The learner centred teaching approach** is the philosophy which underpins this book. Everything in the learning cycle comes back to the learner. Learner centred teaching is a process of developing learning approaches which will work for identified learners in the context in which they have chosen to learn. Every decision about learning is based on these learner needs. Specifically in the online classroom, decisions are made about the teaching approach based on what will help learners to access learning most successfully.
- **Read on** to find out more about all these aspects of online learning. This book offers analysis of learning issues online and strategies for managing them. Additionally, examples and resources are provided to inspire you to think about the potential of web conferencing as a learning space for you and your learners.

2 Getting started

Going into a virtual classroom for the first time is a bit like venturing into a new country. Careful planning and preparation underpin most successful journeys to unfamiliar places and they will also help to ensure that a live online learning event is worthwhile for participants and a satisfying experience for the facilitator. This chapter covers the things that you need to do before you meet with learners in a virtual classroom. It will help you to:

- prepare to teach in a virtual classroom
- explore the technology
- plan for live online learning
- build your confidence as a facilitator.

Preparing to teach in a virtual classroom

Chapter 1 highlighted the potential for live online learning to engage learners by encouraging interaction, discussion and other learner centred approaches. These approaches fit well with what we know about how people learn. For example, we know that people learn best when they are motivated, actively involved, appropriately challenged and supported, have opportunities for dialogue and discussion, and receive feedback. It is also important to take account of what learners already know, consider their needs and preferences, and encourage them to become autonomous and independent. An effective learner centred approach encompasses all these ideas and could include the following strategies:

- The use of group work, discussion, role play or problem based strategies to encourage collaboration and cooperation. Presentation, demonstration or other methods that involve the transmission of information are given less emphasis.
- A willingness to involve learners in making decisions and choices about their learning. Learners might be given options on practical issues such as the time and place of learning, on the strategies and activities used to support learning, or on the nature of assessment.
- An approach to planning that begins with what learners can achieve rather than with what the facilitator will do during a course or lesson. At

the same time the possibility must be kept in mind that what learners learn may be something entirely unpredicted.

- A tutoring strategy that regards the facilitator as a member of the learning community. The facilitator should be able to draw on the expertise that participants bring with them and guide them towards appropriate resources and activities.

There are benefits to the facilitator and learners if a learner centred approach can be adopted. However, it is not unusual for facilitators to revert to teacher led strategies during early experiences in a virtual classroom. New facilitators, when taken outside their normal comfort zone, may find it reassuring to plan a live online session in which the focus is on the delivery of content to learners. This allows them to retain control over the features of the technology that are used and limits the challenges that might arise. This approach may reflect a lack of confidence with the technology, anxieties about facilitating in a virtual classroom, or simply a lack of exposure to what is possible. It may have a place in some contexts, but is not the best way to make use of all the opportunities provided by a virtual classroom. In this example a student identifies some of the problems.

> I was looking forward to the session with the trainer and I had reorganised meetings and made special childcare arrangements so that I could be online. But the session was a complete waste of time. The trainer took about ten minutes to get set up – he was having problems uploading his presentation, it seemed to be in the wrong format – then all he did was show slides full of text and talk at us. He didn't ask us why we were there or what we wanted to know, and since most of the content was already familiar I really didn't get anything at all out of the session. When he asked if there were any questions at the end of his presentation, there was no response, so at least we finished early. I wondered if anyone else was still there or if they had gone off to make a cup of tea or check their email.

Compare that experience with what happened to a student whose tutor took a more interactive approach.

> As soon as we arrived in the virtual classroom the lecturer asked us to type into the chat tool some information about where we were and why we had enrolled on the course. It was really good to learn a bit about everyone else in the group before we started. I hadn't realised that there was

someone else who does the same job as me, it will be helpful to talk to him again. The slides were great. There were lots of interesting graphics and questions for us to think about. It wasn't like listening to a lecture, I had to think on my feet. I was typing things onto the screen or into the chat box and voting on questions every few minutes. I was able to type a question into the chat and was really pleased when it was answered. I thought that my question would have been forgotten as soon as it disappeared up the screen. The time just flew past and although I made some notes I will go back to the recording of the session to check some of the details.

This second example illustrates the ability of a facilitator to use well chosen strategies and activities, in combination with appropriate technical tools, to engage and motivate learners. Adopting a similar learner centred approach that meets learners' needs and encourages interaction and engagement will promote effective learning in a virtual classroom.

Learner centred ideas are a feature of theoretical models of teaching and learning which are relevant to teaching in a virtual classroom. These include the conversational framework (Laurillard, 2002) and community of inquiry model (Garrison, Anderson and Archer, 2000). Whilst careful study of these ideas will benefit any teacher or trainer, they will not always be at the front of a facilitator's mind whilst they are teaching. Instead facilitators rely on personal theories of practice, developed through experience, to inform their actions and help them operate intuitively in the classroom.

If teaching in a virtual classroom follows substantive experience in another teaching context, such as a face to face classroom, personal theories may be challenged and a re-evaluation of teaching actions and beliefs about learning may be needed. For example, in a virtual classroom there is an absence of visual feedback about how learners feel or whether they are engaged. This can be unsettling if you are used to assessing reactions instinctively with a glance around the room. It may cause you to question 'taken for granted' assumptions about using particular approaches. As you can no longer rely on facial expressions or body language to let you know how learners are responding, you have to adapt your practice to include specific requests for feedback. Strategies for obtaining feedback that were formerly intuitive have to be re-evaluated and made explicit so that they can be adapted to the online environment. This also applies to other aspects of learner centred practice. The strategies used to achieve particular outcomes may need to be reassessed in the virtual classroom. Reflection on personal experiences and careful evaluation of what works and what is challenging, supported by revisiting theoretical ideas relevant to your own context, will help you to implement an effective learner centred approach.

Many of the chapters that follow provide examples of learner centred strategies, and we aim to inspire you to adapt these and develop your own approaches for live online learning. However, designing effective activities is not sufficient. A facilitator also requires a good knowledge of the web conferencing environment to understand what is possible and should be confident with the tools available to support the implementation of activities.

Exploring the technology

Becoming familiar with the tools available in a virtual classroom and acquiring sufficient confidence to use them in a live teaching situation are important first steps for most facilitators. Many of the tools available may be familiar to you from other commonly used technologies. For example a chat tool is relatively similar whether it is within a virtual learning environment, virtual classroom or social networking system. The tools for audio or video may be similar to those in systems such as Skype or Facetime. Other tools may be new, for example whiteboard tools, those for application sharing or using breakout rooms. The technical skills that need to be developed will be different for every facilitator, but the strategies used to find out more about them may be similar. In addition to the advice given in this book, some of the opportunities available are to:

- undertake formal training within your own organisation or from another provider
- engage with online training resources such as videos and user manuals
- cultivate 'expert friends', for example educational technologists, who can support you in person or answer questions by email
- experiment and practice on your own or with others whenever possible for meetings, discussions and other events
- shadow more experienced facilitators and engage in conversation about how they do things in their virtual classrooms.

As well as being able to use the tools within the software there may be learning required to ensure that you can create and set up virtual classrooms appropriately. Separate virtual classrooms may be needed for different functions, groups or time periods. You may need to ensure that only certain students have access to particular spaces. In all cases you will need to make your classrooms easy for your learners to find and access.

The technology survival kit

It is not necessary to know everything about the technology in order to get started as a facilitator, although, as Salmon (2011) suggests in her extensive work on developing e-moderators for online discussion, you should be comfortable and familiar with the technology and aware of the strengths and weaknesses of the software you use. Our suggested list of the features you need to find and practice in order to get started is presented below. We focus on the tools you need to communicate with your learners, and those you need to share materials on the whiteboard so that these can be used as a stimulus for discussion or an activity. Other features might be explored later, such as those needed for creating breakout rooms for group work, using voting tools, or sharing applications. These are considered later in this book. Figure 2.1 uses an image of a virtual classroom to indicate where you are likely to find the essential tools, and they are discussed in Table 2.1.

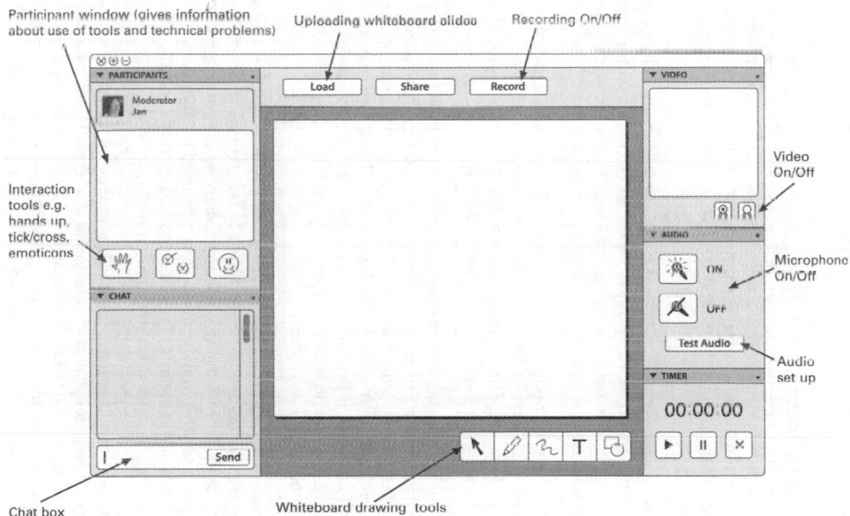

Figure 2.1 Essential virtual classroom tools

Familiarity with the essential web conferencing tools will help you survive your initial journey into the virtual classroom. Later chapters introduce other tools that can be explored as you travel into some of the more remote and specialised terrain.

Table 2.1 Getting started with the essential virtual classroom tools

Tool	What you need to know
Audio set up tools	The facilitator and participants need to ensure that they have microphones and speakers set up optimally before a session starts. Some web conferencing systems may detect your equipment automatically. Ensure you know how this is done so that you can make changes to volume levels and broadcast the best-quality sound possible, and so that you can help learners who are unable to hear or are unsure about setting up their own equipment.
Chat tools	Participants who do not know how to use the microphone, or are initially apprehensive about speaking to an online group, may feel more comfortable with the chat tool. You can use this to communicate with individuals who cannot hear you, and to encourage participants to pose questions, post responses to your questions and interact with each other. Check that you know how to send messages to the whole group and find out how to send private messages to individual participants or other facilitators.
Talk/video	There may be limits to the number of participants who can have audio or video switched on at any one time, and as facilitator you may have some control over this. Find out how to enable one, two or more microphones or web cams. Experiment to find out whether it is best to take turns with the microphone or more appropriate to leave them all switched on to encourage a more natural conversational style. The video feed may 'follow' the speaker so they are visible when they are speaking. Find out if it is possible to set this up.
Interaction tools	Ensuring that your participants can use the various feedback tools will help you encourage and manage interaction. Find out how participants display a smiley face or a tick or cross so that you can ask them for feedback about how they are feeling or confirmation that they understand what you have asked them to do. You should be able to demonstrate appropriate use of these tools and know how to clear participants' selections or help them do this. The raised-hand tool will help you manage discussions and in some systems the first participant to raise their hand will move to the top of the list. Setting protocols for the use of the 'away' tool, for example during breaks or if there are distractions, will make sure that you know who is listening and engaged. You may need to model appropriate use of tools for interaction to encourage participants to engage fully with them.
Whiteboard	Although you may wish to start a session with a blank whiteboard, a slide could be displayed to provide a focus and stimulus for discussion. Find out how to prepare and upload a slide and use the pointer tool to direct participants' attention to particular areas of the screen. If you and your participants are comfortable with the whiteboard drawing and writing tools this creates a wide range of opportunities for annotating material or creating new resources. The whiteboard tools can be used for summarising comments from a discussion, creating mind maps, collating answers to a question or drawing diagrams. The option to add graphics and clip art may be available. These tools are well worth exploring as they provide opportunities to support creative and engaging activities.
Recording tools	You may or may not wish to generate recordings of sessions for learners to revisit, but it will be useful to know how these tools work so that you can make recordings for your own use. Viewing a recording of a session will support evaluation and development of your own practice. It may be possible to record elements of a session as well as the whole experience. For example some web conferencing software allows whiteboard screens or chat transcripts to be saved independently. Participants will appreciate you making these resources available to them, and will also benefit from knowing know how to create them themselves. It may be necessary to negotiate with participants or formalise a policy on the use of recordings before you begin to share recorded elements of your sessions.

Dealing with technical challenges

Technical support personnel may (or may not) be available to help you set up and become familiar with web conferencing software. An absence of appropriate support to help you get to know some of the technical aspects of your web conferencing system will make it difficult to develop or sustain successful learning. The following cautionary tale illustrates some of the problems of 'going it alone'.

> We tried to use some web conferencing on one course, but gave up after a couple of disastrous trial attempts. There were all sorts of things we didn't know about – how to sort out echoes and buffering delays that were caused by everyone having their microphone on at once and using integral computer speakers that created feedback. We tried to use too many video cameras at once and didn't really grasp the screen layout conventions or know how to resize windows or move them about. We thought we could just turn up and start and didn't appreciate the need for sorting out sound levels and default input and output devices, as well as getting everyone settled online first. You name it, we stumbled over it

This facilitator acknowledged that when she started with web conferencing 'she didn't know what she didn't know'. Learning how to use the software took self-belief and perseverance. She had to pick herself up in the face of challenges, learn the lessons they provided, and try again. Learning how to use web conferencing does not have to be such a painful process and will be easier if you can find appropriately experienced technical support as well as expert friends and mentors.

It is important to remember, too, that learning how to use the technology is not a one-time event for any web conferencing user. A new software interface can temporarily puzzle even a highly experienced facilitator. The first meeting with a diverse international class or the presence of a student with particular needs can bring to the surface unexpected issues that could not be anticipated. In the context of constant technological change a facilitator needs to aim to develop:

- confidence with the basic features and functions of the software
- resilience and adaptability to deal with new versions and features
- a willingness to learn and relearn when new features become available
- creativity and flexibility to deal with or work around technical issues which arise

- an ability to establish appropriate support systems, mentors and other expert friends.

All facilitators make mistakes with the technology, especially during their first few sessions. During some of his early experiences Bower (2011) identified that his ability with web conferencing software had an impact on the effectiveness of learning. He misused the technology in a number of ways, in some cases because he was not aware of what learners could see, and he felt he was unable to advise students on what actions to take. He also made mistakes, such as posting private messages to a public chat. Other facilitators report making errors too.

> The frequency with which I forgot to put on my microphone, and alternatively forgot to put off my microphone and heavy breathed into it until my co-facilitator told me I was doing that, made me really grateful that I had her there when I was learning to use the system. I've now got the confidence to say to participants 'if I do something silly with my microphone will you please tell me'.

There are many technical challenges that can arise whilst you are facilitating learning in a virtual classroom, but it is worth remembering that your learners cannot necessarily tell if you are struggling to remember how to perform a particular task or getting stressed out by the technology. Often the best response to a mistake with the technology is to move on quickly without making too big an issue of it. Just make a note to check the issue out later. The facilitator quoted above benefited from having a co-facilitator available to help during the first few sessions, and her comments also highlight the need for facilitators to have the confidence to ask participants for help with technical issues. This is part of the resilience and flexibility needed.

Other practical measures can be taken to help with some of the issues that may be encountered. For example, you can be logged into a session as a student at the same time as being logged in as a facilitator to get a clearer picture of what students are experiencing. Some users advocate having a second screen available so that they can keep an eye on the 'student view'. The fact that most facilitators will make mistakes, particularly during early sessions, suggests that tutors should avoid trying to retain complete control over the virtual classroom. Instead they should acknowledge the skills and experience that may be present within a group of learners, and use this to benefit everyone. A calm, positive approach will reassure your learners even if behind the scenes you are flustered or anxious. Planning and practising for learning events so that you do not take yourself beyond your technical ability is important. At the same time, in order to develop your practice, you should build in opportunities that allow you to gradually extend your technical skills and increase your expertise as a facilitator.

Planning for live online learning

A plan of some sort guides most tutors and trainers as they deliver a learning experience. This may be a comprehensive lesson plan, or a few hastily written notes, depending on the context and requirements. Some web conferencing systems offer sophisticated planning tools that aim to help with the structure and preparation of learning events. They can support the facilitator by allowing the advance preparation of whiteboard screens and individual tools. They may be particularly useful where a team of facilitators deliver similar sessions on different occasions, but are not always necessary. An alternative low-tech approach which permits flexibility and offers support whilst you are delivering a session is to include information about the tools required in your plan for the event. Table 2.2 provides an example of one such 'extended' plan. This was used to guide facilitators before and during a session which was part of a lecturer training course. Including details of the tools that are required during the session allowed new facilitators to focus on these and practice before going live. It also provided a useful checklist of the technical skills that learners required.

In this hour long session a wide range of tools has been used – audio and text tools, interaction tools, whiteboard and drawing tools, and the timer. The facilitator needs to be comfortable with these before they start and able to support learners who are unsure or make mistakes. Leaving microphones on after speaking is a common error which can impact on audio quality for all by introducing background noise or echoes. Facilitators need to establish protocols for speaking, and model good practice themselves.

As well as highlighting the technical tools needed, the plan in Table 2.2 includes a range of activities and strategies designed to encourage interaction and help promote successful learner centred strategies in the virtual classroom. It provides opportunities for learners to raise issues of concern so that their needs can be addressed. It will also reveal evidence about their technical competence and confidence. This might be especially helpful where learners have particular needs or characteristics that require consideration. For example a dyslexic learner or someone with physical limitations who is new to the environment may need time to become familiar with the tools before the strategies that are most helpful for them can be identified. As suggested on a web site promoting technology for inclusion, technology

Table 2.2 Extract from a lesson plan including information about web conferencing tools

Time	Activity	Tutor needs to	Learners need to
30 mins before start time	**Welcome and getting started**	Upload whiteboard slides. Display slide 1 (reminder to participants to test their audio set up).	Test audio set up. Use audio/chat tools for informal chat.
15 mins	**Introductory activity:** collaboratively drawing a diagram	Display slide 2 with instructions. Check that learners know how to use appropriate whiteboard drawing tools. Invite questions using hand-raise. Set timer to 4 minutes. Invite feedback using emoticons or tick and cross. (Was it fun or confusing? Are you comfortable with using the whiteboard tools now?)	Use whiteboard tools to draw lines, shapes, add colours etc. Provide peer support through text or audio. Raise hand. Use emoticons and tick/cross.
15 mins	**Reporting on progress:** individuals give a brief report in turn	Display slide 3 'Which activities have you found interesting, challenging or helpful this week?' Ask learners to raise their hand when they are ready to contribute. Use the order created to invite contributions by audio or text. Invite contribution and questions from those not speaking in the chat box. Monitor chat box for questions.	Raise hand. Use audio/chat tool.
10 mins	**Whole-group discussion activity:** What is guidance?	Display slide 4 'What is guidance?' Invite contributions and record these using whiteboard writing tools (If group is large, invite a student to act as scribe).	Use audio/chat tool. Raise hand to make contributions. Scribe will need confidence with whiteboard writing tools.

has the potential to liberate such learners, but without careful planning can instead make it exclusive and restricted (JISC TechDis, 2013).

Putting together appropriate plans requires an awareness of what can be done with web conferencing, as well as imagination and creativity. The next section considers some of the ways in which you can develop an appreciation of what is possible with web conferencing.

Developing confidence as a facilitator

Since the majority of facilitators have only limited experience of being learners in virtual classrooms, one of the best ways to develop an understanding of what works and what does not work is to enrol in classes, courses and webinars. This tutor found an opportunity to be a 'test student' very helpful.

> When I started I had a lot of experience using text based discussions, but that's a very different experience from being a facilitator of live online learning. When I was preparing to tutor, I was privileged to have been invited to some sessions where more experienced facilitators were testing out different activities. So before I was using it for my own teaching, I had the experience of being a participant in activities that were being developed. I think that's important – you have to understand what it's like to be a participant before you start using web conferencing as a tutor.

Trialling activities with colleagues is one opportunity to be a participant, but it is even better to engage fully in an online class. If it is not possible to join in sessions run by others at your own institution, software vendors frequently run marketing and promotional webinars, and many professional training organisations run live online sessions. Take as many opportunities as you can to engage as a learner as this will give you the opportunity to reflect on your experiences. After each session ask yourself questions such as:

- Did you feel part of the class?
- Were you able to interact?
- How did learners from other backgrounds or contexts get on during the session?
- Were any problems or issues you faced addressed?
- What strategies or resources that the facilitator used did you particularly like (or dislike)?

Talking to colleagues and other students, and reading the growing literature on learners' experiences, will also provide an insight into what it is like to be a learner. Here is an example of the experiences of a tutor relatively new to web conferencing who was exploring the possibilities of the technology by engaging in a wide variety of live online learning opportunities.

I was amazed when I logged on for an international session led by a facilitator in the US and there were over four hundred participants. 'Wow,' was my first thought, 'how will he manage this?' Unsurprisingly, none of the students were able to use microphones – only the speaker and moderator had access to these tools. The session was cleverly designed around lots of questions to allow us to interact with the chat tool. It was a bit overwhelming to see over four hundred responses to a question requiring a numerical answer scrolling rapidly up the screen, but this did at least give a sense of what the audience were thinking. I remember thinking that I would find this a very difficult situation to facilitate. How could you identify anyone having problems? How could you respond to an individual? I also took away from the session the value of using lots of questions to promote engagement and interaction – that was a useful lesson.

Another way to develop strategies and approaches that are successful in a virtual classroom is to take on the role of an apprentice. Traditionally an apprentice was one who learned a trade or craft over a period of time under the guidance of a highly skilled expert. This concept is a useful one to apply to becoming a web conferencing facilitator. The value of embracing an apprentice role alongside a more experienced peer is that it may help manage initial anxieties, provide ideas about effective strategies, and provide reassurance that the tools are being used appropriately. Having someone else present in the first few sessions you facilitate, for example to handle technical issues that arise, to respond to any unexpected events or to chase up non-attenders, can be tremendously helpful. It may be appropriate, if resources allow, to have a second facilitator present at the start of all sessions, or to adopt a co-tutoring approach whilst skills and confidence to 'go it alone' are developed.

Most new facilitators will not be starting completely from scratch. They will bring with them previous teaching experiences and a certain level of technological competence and confidence. Hopefully, they will also be open to new ideas and willing to take a few risks. Guidance from an expert, through shadowing or observation of live sessions, discussions of practice and problems, and engagement in training opportunities, will help an experienced tutor or trainer to quickly adapt their practice to an online classroom. Suggestions for other strategies for developing confidence as a facilitator are provided in Table 2.3.

In the chapters which follow there are many examples of activities that can be undertaken in a virtual classroom, along with evidence of learners' experiences of these. Supplementing these with hands-on experience as a

Table 2.3 Strategies for developing confidence as a facilitator of live online learning

Strategy	Details
Be a learner	Participate as a learner in small and large group settings, for instance webinars, training courses, discussions and meetings, to find out what is possible and help you evaluate what you think works best.
Shadow	Shadow or observe more experienced colleagues and engage in discussion about their strategies and practices.
Reflect	Reflect on the strategies you use in other contexts and consider whether these could be replicated in or adapted for a virtual classroom.
Facilitate	Offer to co-facilitate part of a session for a more experienced colleague or act as a second moderator. You could, for example, moderate the chat stream during a large group session. Take the opportunity to de-brief and reflect on your experiences with your colleague.
Gain diverse experiences	Use web conferencing in different contexts and for different purposes. Experiencing live online meetings, interviews, or supervision sessions will help you develop confidence with the tools.
Evaluate	Review recordings of your own sessions, or those of other tutors, and evaluate your practice.

learner or as an apprentice facilitator will give you a much clearer insight into what will work best in your own context and help you prepare for successful live online learning.

IN SUMMARY

This chapter has introduced some of the issues that need to be considered in order to prepare for teaching in a virtual classroom.

- **Planning for a learner centred approach**: in a virtual classroom a learner centred approach works best, so sessions should be planned to include activities and resources which support engaging, interactive sessions and allow you to be responsive to learners' needs. There is more advice on possible activities and strategies in the chapters that follow.
- **Developing confidence with essential web conferencing tools**: the most important tools in the virtual classroom are the ones that facilitate basic communication and interaction – the audio, text,

video and whiteboard tools. Becoming familiar with these before meeting learners is important; it is helpful to plan which you will use and practice with them.

- **Preparing to teach in a virtual classroom**: a number of suggestions have been made, including engaging as a learner, shadowing experienced colleagues, undertaking formal training and learning through practice. Preparation could include reflection on experiences in other contexts and needs to be undertaken with a willingness to re-examine your assumptions and beliefs about teaching and learning.

With appropriate preparations made you are ready to embark on your journey into your virtual classroom, appropriately set up and equipped. However, before you can facilitate learning further attention needs to be paid to your learners. Who are they and how should they be prepared? The next chapter takes a closer look at learners, as a better understanding of your participants will help you provide effective support as part of a learner centred approach to successful live online learning.

3 Welcoming learners

Knowing about learners' needs and expectations can help tutors and trainers to create a welcoming learning experience which motivates learners and increases their enjoyment of live online learning. This chapter develops this theme of motivation and building the confidence of online learners, covering the following topics:

- the experience of being an online learner
- getting to know online learners
- online learners and technology
- the significance of learner location
- supporting new online learners
- making learners feel welcome online
- helping learners to connect with one another online.

The experience of being an online learner

People behave in different ways when they are online. Some people are very open in their online communication, for example offering personal information on social networking sites and sharing photos of their family. Some people are more elusive and avoid posting messages, but enjoy looking at messages posted by other people. Similarly, learners operate in different ways in the virtual classroom. Here are three learners' descriptions of their early web conferencing experiences.

> First of all, I need to feel welcomed, so that I have a sense of belonging to the online community. I probably approach the online situation with certain anxieties – will I manage the technology, will I succeed in learning, how will I manage relationships? Some reassurance therefore is necessary in terms of preparation for online learning – having as much information as possible about what the environment will be like and what will be expected of me will help. I am happy to work in a group and collaborate with others, and I enjoy the creative effect of multiple ideas.

I love the anonymity of online learning. I tend to be slow to participate and if I do participate, I need to have my comments validated in some way. I go quiet if I feel that I'm out of step with the ideas being discussed. Surprisingly, I listen very well online and think carefully about what others say. My contributions can be more focused because I have to wait to have my say and I like this. I can lose interest if facilitators talk all the time or have irritating mannerisms. I'm also quite intolerant of apologies, feeling that the leader of the session should either make things work or move on. I've just re-read this and think I might be quite a difficult student!

I was very timid in my first few live online sessions. Most of these were webinars and I didn't know anyone else in the audience, so I just listened and watched how other people were interacting. After a couple of sessions I gained the confidence to type in the odd text message, but I was always a bit nervous in case I was exposing my ignorance or asking a silly question. A really interesting early experience was being in an audience of hundreds for an online training event. It was a very interactive session and participants were encouraged to use the text chat to interact. Watching text messages whizz on to the screen was fascinating and I was delighted when someone replied directly to one of my contributions! The text chat is a good way for me to contribute – I'd rather type in a response to a question than be put on the spot to answer verbally.

Some of the insecurity felt by these learners would be the same in any learning situation, but the accounts reveal particular concerns about the newness of the virtual classroom environment. They also demonstrate how learners' behaviour may be influenced by how they cope with the technology and the online learning environment. In the virtual classroom someone who avoids communication on a social networking site may enjoy the anonymity of the chat box, whilst another learner may relish the opportunity to interact using audio and web cam functions. As tutors or trainers, it is important for us to remember how we felt as novice online learners and to acknowledge differences in our behaviour in different online settings. This helps us to understand the actions and concerns of our learners. We are less likely to make assumptions about the way they behave online if we remember how we felt when everything was new. It may surprise you to learn that the three learners who described their initial experiences of live online learning are now experienced online tutors.

▶ Getting to know online learners

Spending time finding out all you can about your learners will help you to respond to their needs and successfully manage interaction online. The cues we use to support communication in face to face encounters are often absent online. Voices in a virtual classroom, like handwriting on a page, can be confusing or deceptive.

Information about online learners can be gained from the same sources as learners in other educational settings. If they are available, course application forms may provide basic information about age, gender, occupation, educational experience and any learning support needs. Even where there is no formal application, some information can be gathered during the recruitment process. Recruitment by email, for example, will target people with a known interest in the subject or a certain professional profile. Colleagues who have worked with similar groups of learners may be another source of background information, as are published case studies and research reports.

Any assumptions we make should be open to review when we find out more about individual learners, but we have found that most people who sign up for a course which is delivered online have some computer skills and a belief that they can manage the online learning experience. Similarly, they are likely to have expectations that there will be technical support and they will only be required to use additional computing skills if these can be taught during the course. Someone who has chosen a course with synchronous online meetings is also likely to favour working with others, or at least have a preference for meeting their tutor and engaging in facilitated learning, rather than working alone. The assumption made here, however, is that the learners have *chosen* an online course – some may not have a choice if their employer or their circumstances mean that no other option is available.

Learners themselves are, perhaps, the most reliable source of information, although some learners prefer not to reveal too much about their situation, experience or beliefs. It may be that they are able to do this more easily online than in a face to face meeting and this may be a reason for choosing online learning. It is particularly helpful to have some kind of dialogue with individuals by phone or online before they start a course, if this is possible. It is also useful to use email to send a warm introductory message to participants who have enrolled for a course, encouraging them to reply and provide some information about themselves. It is best at this stage to limit requests for information to very simple questions about their experience with technology and learning preferences.

Although learners are the best source of information, it may be important for them to review their assumptions about themselves and about learning, particularly learning online. Adults can have some fixed views about themselves as learners that are difficult to shift, such as 'I'm no good at maths,' or 'I'm hopeless at writing essays'. These fixed views can give a false impression about their abilities, motivation and what we can expect from them.

It may be valuable to know different things about learners at different times during an online course. Asking direct questions to elicit information can be perceived as intrusive or inappropriate during early online sessions, so it is useful to decide what you need to know and to use a range of techniques to gather insights. Engaging in informal chat before sessions or during breaks can be helpful, but more formal strategies can also be used. These should be meaningful to learners as well as useful for you. For example, activities which encourage reflective practice on learning skills and habits can be built into online sessions to reveal more about learners. In the 'You as a learner' activity shown in Figures 3.1 and 3.2, learners were asked to view a slide containing

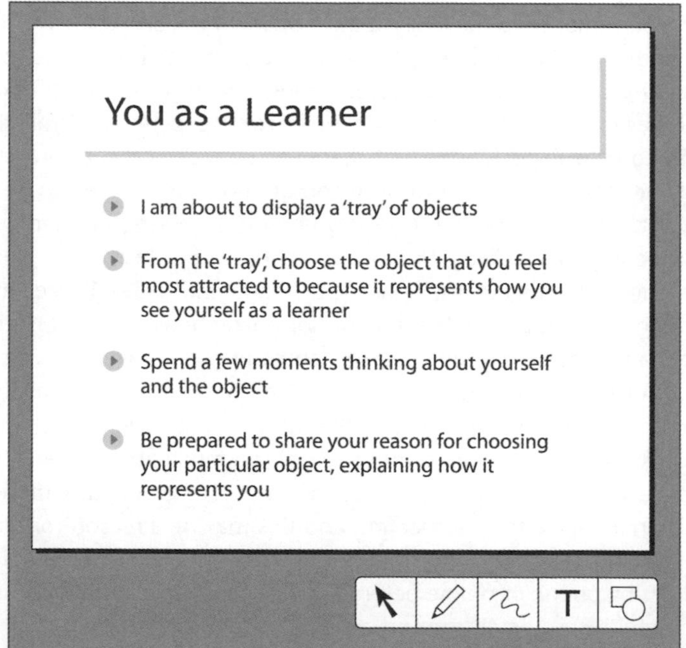

Figure 3.1 Instruction slide for 'You as a learner' activity

Figure 3.2 Images of objects used for 'You as a learner' activity

pictures of a range of objects and select one which they felt represented how they saw themselves as a learner.

Once an object had been selected learners were asked to explain their choice. The examples of learner responses to this activity provided useful insights for both learner and tutor.

> "I'm a butterfly – always flitting around different resources, seeing what's there but moving on quickly."

> "I'm a magnifying glass, focusing on the detail, checking out that what I'm seeing means what it seems to mean."

> "The spinning top sums it up for me. Always in a flap, rushing around – even making a lot of noise to draw attention to how busy I am flapping around!"

Collating comments such as those in the quotes from learners can reveal much about learning preferences and challenges and is a helpful reflective exercise for both learners and facilitators. This can be useful in the early stages of a course, but also when learners return to study after a break, or if there are signs that they are losing their way with the course work.

By getting to know learners' preferences and challenges, there is more chance of offering appropriate support and encouragement. By knowing about their background and experience, the risk of encountering difficult situations is reduced and the opportunity to build on learners' past experiences is enhanced.

Online learners and technology

Learners' confidence and their ability to work with technology may influence their feelings about working online. It may be a more difficult experience if a learner is anxious about the technology or frustrated by technical problems. Their goodwill may be lost if they find that they are frequently making mistakes and feel embarrassed about their inability to get things right. It is very important that learners are not alienated in the early stages by unclear instructions or flippant comments about how easy it is to carry out a particular task in the virtual classroom. To avoid this, it is helpful to offer regular reminders of how to do things and ask participants to acknowledge that they understand what they have to do. Even if basic training has been carried out during induction, it is important to be aware of the need to refresh everyone's memory.

Not all learners will be anxious about technology. Valaitis et al. (2007) identified three perspectives on technology amongst health sciences students. Some were 'pragmatists' who, although they may have preferred face to face sessions, valued the flexibility of web conferencing and were realistic about problems and technical difficulties. The second group were termed 'positive communicators'. These learners generally enjoyed new technology and valued web conferencing for the opportunities it provided for communication in different contexts. Thirdly, 'shy enthusiasts' were people who were comfortable with technology, did not feel disadvantaged by the lack of nonverbal communication features and preferred web conferencing to face to face sessions. Classifications such as these are a useful starting point for understanding a new group of learners, or when working with a large group. Considering the support needs of these three types, rather than individual learners, may be a practical approach for a busy facilitator.

Learners' attitudes to technology may also give some clues to how they feel about learning in general. Online learners are asked to tackle new information and ideas relating to their course but also to manage complex technology. It is a dual learning experience which can be stressful and also underestimated in terms of the impact on overall success in the course. Motivation plays an important role in learner resilience in this complex environment and can differ greatly for individual learners in a group. It can also vary for an individual during a period of study, but motivation generally is most likely to be high if the learning experience is enjoyable and valuable. Rogers (2002) suggests that motivation is related to a number of factors, including inner needs, interaction, prior learning and personal goals. Many people who sign up for an online course or training session do so for pragmatic reasons. They may not be able to take time away from work or family to attend a course. Their motivation to learn may be intrinsic, based on a desire to learn or to better themselves through education and gaining qualifications, but their choice of study method may be determined by practical considerations rather than choice. The extrinsic motivation that is likely to keep them on course may come from employers or other external factors, but most importantly will come from the quality of the online learning experience.

The stimulation that comes from being with others online and engaging in activities can lead to a psychological arousal that is in itself motivating (Hrastinski, 2008). This can be seen in game shows on television or even quizzes in the classroom. If learners seem to lack motivation, involving them in activities that produce speedy responses, and even rewards, may help to foster a stronger commitment to learning. Feedback can include positive rewards, such as a 'thumbs up' icon, or a round of applause, or simply the approval of the facilitator or others in the group. All these approaches can make online learners feel more confident and perhaps motivate them to become more proactive in their online interactions.

However, some learners choose an online course deliberately because they believe it will involve less interaction with others, less time wasted with discussion and collaboration. They may 'just want to get on with it' believing there is a quick way to pass and get a desired qualification. This suggests that information about online courses needs to be very clear – learners need to be able to find out what to expect – so that they are signing up for an experience which meets their needs and are not demotivated by the reality of encountering something different.

It is helpful to use every opportunity to gather information about learners, including documentation, informal chat and activities during online sessions. This information can be particularly valuable when planning how to make use of the different tools available in the virtual classroom, and so ensure that the learning experience is as good as it can be.

▶ The significance of learner location

Learners take part in live online sessions from a variety of locations, including homes, offices, public places like cafes and airports, and perhaps even whilst on holiday. This flexibility allows learners to participate when otherwise it might have been impossible. It can also be very convenient to study from home or to study at a particular time of day or night that suits these locations. Finding out where participants are at the start of a session by asking them to indicate their location on a map is useful for learners and facilitators, providing prompts for interaction and helping people relax and feel part of a learning group. 'How's the weather in Portugal?' may not seem like the most academic one liner to start a tutorial, but if it gets everyone talking, or provides a theme to make people laugh throughout the session, then it is a valuable chat line.

The flexibility of being able to log in from anywhere may be a benefit of live online learning, but it may also constrain learners. It may be difficult to focus on a session in a noisy office environment, or embarrassing to be seen speaking into a computer when sitting in an airport lounge. In hushed tones, one of our students said that he was in a library so most of his communication would be in the chat box. In a course which requires discussion of personal experiences or participants' professional contexts, being in a work location may prevent them from sharing a story or example, or inhibit honest and open reflection on work related issues.

It can be helpful to advise learners to consider their study location and to establish a simple code of practice if topics to be discussed need to be confidential to the group. Learners should be advised to engage with sessions from a location where they will feel relaxed and where there are few distractions and interruptions. Some learners will prefer their home environment where they have peace and quiet and home comforts, but others may have to make decisions about where to participate based on the availability of a computer or internet access. Some learners have been found to make decisions based on where they have more control over the technology (Cornelius, 2013a). For example, working on a laptop at home means that the constraints of a network system can be avoided. Even when an appropriate environment is identified there may still be distractions – children in the house, dogs barking, the doorbell ringing and other less predictable interruptions. Discussing some of the issues associated with study location with learners can provide a useful topic of conversation and allow you to be helpful in terms of offering support. As always, care must be taken to avoid straying into private territory. It may seem like an amusing icebreaker to ask everyone to describe what they are wearing or the room they are sitting in, only to find some participants definitely do not want to share this information.

The flexibility of 'anywhere' engagement in live online learning means that participants can be globally distributed. The following example shows some of the complexity of this flexibility for an online tutor.

> My students were based in different countries and also different time zones. The difference in time was a particular issue for some of them. Every Friday at 6 in the morning, their time, some of them logged into the online session, but for me it was early evening of the previous day!

Awareness of time zone differences may help you to understand learners' behaviour, for example, diagnosing an absence resulting from errors in time conversion. However, time differences are only one aspect of the international virtual classroom. Sensitivity to different cultures and use of language can be very important. Conversely, learners who live in a different country from the course provider may not understand local references, or even know where the course is coming from. Knowing about our learners' location means that we can be sensitive to cultural differences and understanding of learners who live or work in different countries.

Supporting new online learners

If things go badly in the virtual classroom, new online learners can become demotivated very quickly. Many learners will be nervous or lack confidence. This difficulty was identified by Vitartas, Rowe and Ellis (2008) amongst business students using web conferencing for the first time. For most courses some sort of orientation or induction is provided to help learners feel confident about their course. It allows them to gain confidence when using online tools and makes them aware of the things that might happen so that they know what to do if any problems occur. Induction is also an important opportunity to inspire and engage learners.

If there is an opportunity to bring learners together face to face before meeting online, this can help them to get to know one another and learn how to use the technology. Taking a group photograph as a reminder of group members can be useful and provide a starting point for the first online session. The photograph can be displayed and participants invited to write their name beside their picture. It can also be used in later sessions as part of an activity or in a welcome message to give a sense of group identity.

If induction has to be completed totally online, then different strategies are needed to make participants feel at ease with their group, their tutor and the technology. A strategy we found useful was to ask learners to write down three things they would like their tutor to know about them as they start the course. This was returned confidentially by email and followed by a chat with the tutor on the phone or online. This approach gives learners the opportunity to express their feelings about being a learner and give factual information about other commitments or specific learning needs. Here are some examples of comments made by learners when asked to write confidentially at the induction about things they wanted the tutor to know about them.

> “I want to get this qualification as quickly as possible. I know I have to study but I have a busy social life and play sport competitively, so have to spend several evenings during the week training. I was easily bored at school and worry that I'll find this course boring. My job involves using computers and I think I can manage the online technology very easily. I also use social networks and the internet frequently. I need interesting things to do during online sessions so that I don't lose interest.”

> “My family do not approve of me studying. They believe it is not appropriate for a woman like me to try to better herself through education.”

> “I have to get up at 4.30 am to take part in workshops, so may not be the most talkative of your students.”

> “The internet connection can be a problem here. It's very frustrating being cut off in the middle of something important in the session. Can you repeat things if I disappear for a few minutes? The connection seems to come back but it can be a real pain to lose the thread of what's being said.”

All of these responses provide useful information to help the tutor acknowledge the concerns of learners, and give the learners a sense that their needs will be addressed.

Usually it would feel right to describe technology as a tool and not the key to learning. However, putting the learner first in online learning inevitably means giving the technology priority. If there is no transport link to a physical study location, it is unlikely that you will get good attendance: helping students to work with online technology provides the transport link to your course, but they may not just hop aboard! Case studies and descriptions of typical online learners may not capture the complexity and the changeable levels of confidence that learners display. The most difficult students to support are often those with limited computing skills. This is particularly true if they have a general horror of things technical or reject anything new that makes them feel unskilled. At the other end of the spectrum is the technical expert who expects to be able to use the system effortlessly and may be critical if the virtual classroom does not do things as well as other systems.

Induction and orientation activities should provide opportunities to become familiar with the software, but not require a learner to be fully skilled before they embark on their learning. The opportunity to have a trial session, using the technology to interact in an informal setting, rather than at a formal learning event may help learner confidence. Opportunities for peer support and peer tutoring in the use of the tools may also be valuable, and may be particularly useful if learners are reticent about asking tutors for help with skills they feel are not part of academic course requirements. The following accounts of initial experiences with web conferencing technology illustrate these points.

> I was very apprehensive about using the technology. I chose to do the first online session at work so that there would be colleagues around who could help if I got in a muddle. I had a practice session which went very well but on the day of the first workshop, the internet kept going down and I lost my connection. I logged in again each time, but felt that I was bobbing in and out like a yoyo. The tutor said twice, 'Oh, hi, you're back again.' Eventually, it settled down and after the break the tutor reviewed what had been covered when I was away and asked others in the group to give their impressions. Actually, this was really helpful and made me feel quite special. Almost everyone acknowledged how difficult it must have been for me and how helpless you feel when you lose internet connection.

The second example is from someone who felt very comfortable about using the technology.

> I could tell that I was more experienced than others in the group and I felt quite confident about using all the web conferencing tools. I liked the way that the tutor kept reminding everyone what to do and actually made us use the tools rather than just telling us what the buttons were for. Surprisingly, I was the one who got it wrong. The system I've used in the past has a facility for selecting who you want to send chat messages to, but this system didn't look quite the same. I knew someone else in the group and wanted to send her a fun and reassuring message but ended up sending it to the whole group. Thank goodness it was polite! Interestingly, my message to everyone proved quite a success and there were some appreciative replies.

These stories emphasise the importance of preparation, practice and support, all of which can be provided through appropriate induction and orientation activities. It is also important to get to know more about learners than just their ability to work with technology and their confidence as learners. Technology and the use of the internet have revolutionised learning for many people. Online courses provide a valuable opportunity for students with specific learning needs to take part in courses that it may be difficult for them to access locally. For the online tutor or trainer, it can be very difficult to know how to manage the assistive technology used by individual learners and to know how to deal with any disclosed disability or learning issue. At the application stage for a course it is possible to ask about learning support needs, but not all learners choose to disclose their personal circumstances. It is also possible to ask learners about their learning needs before the course starts, but again this can be difficult and embarrassing if questions are unwelcome. Inclusiveness easily becomes intrusiveness if too many questions are asked too early in a relationship with new learners. The suggested use of a private questionnaire at induction asking learners what they want their tutor to know about them, may provide an opportunity for learners to talk about their specific learning needs. Support for dyslexia is often mentioned at this stage, and also personal circumstances at home, such as being a carer or working night shifts. The form could be adapted to ask more probing questions about the need for assistive technology or additional time or support for learning activities.

The focus of all enquiries about learning support should be on the needs of the learner and should respect their right not to declare personal information unless they wish to. As the relationship with learners develops, they may become willing to give more information about their situation and to offer the tutor or trainer help with using specific technology which supports their learning. Other learners may be very open about their support needs, and perhaps even demanding in terms of tutor time and support. Additionally, it may be important to establish how much information learners wish to share with others in the virtual classroom group. This care for individual learners is familiar to most tutors and trainers, the difference online is that there are fewer visual reminders of individuals and their needs, and so it is essential to keep confidential notes and reminders of identified support needs and commitments that you have made to help learners in particular circumstances.

Making learners feel welcome online

Here is another personal account of the experience of being a new online learner, referring to the importance of making learners feel welcome.

> When I first arrived at the online session, I could see my name was on the participant list, but what I appreciated most was being welcomed personally by the tutor. It made all the difference for her to use my name and say 'hello'. She did this with each person as they arrived. I understand that in a very large group this may not be possible, but it allowed me to feel a sense of belonging to the group, and a sense that I was in the right place, that I had a right to be there, and that I was wanted there. When I responded and said 'hello', it was to the tutor and to the others who'd arrived before me, so it was about the whole group, not just the tutor.

In contrast, another online learner described his experience of being in a room with a colleague who was doing the same online course. His colleague had already managed to get into the virtual classroom. He could see on his colleague's computer that the session had started, but he was unable to log in, despite several attempts.

> It was so frustrating, like being on the outside of the classroom door, seeing everyone inside, and not being allowed in! I almost felt like banging my fists on the door and shouting 'let me in'! But of course there was no door only an internet connection that wouldn't connect.

Welcoming online learners is about making learners feel that they are in the right place and that they have a right to be there. Feeling welcome in any situation is about a variety of sensory clues. When we visit someone in person, they may say welcoming things, but if there is no smile to accompany their words we sense that it is not a good time to call. If we have been invited somewhere, our feeling of being welcome is often associated with how prepared for our visit our host seems to be, maybe drinks laid out, or the warmth of lights or a fire. Similarly in a classroom teaching situation, a tutor may prepare the room by organising seating, displaying visual clues about the lesson, preparing name labels or ensuring handouts are ready for each learner. The tutor's readiness to lead an online training session should also be evident as participants arrive. They are more likely to feel welcome if they are greeted individually by a tutor who is available to them – just as our learner described above.

It can make a real difference to the success of an online course if some thought is given to the first impression the learners will get of the tutor, and also to the routines and ways of working that the tutor wants to establish. First impressions count. Online we make quick decisions about where we will direct our attention. This is a common experience when shopping online or when looking for information. If you are looking for an internet video clip to show you how to carry out a task, such as cooking or making something, the attitude and approach of the presenter may influence which video you choose to view. You may give each clip only a few seconds' attention before moving on. The significance of these first impressions can be intimidating for an online tutor or trainer. We may ask ourselves, 'How long will learners give me before they switch off?'

The answer lies in having a purpose and plan for the online session which focuses on the learners' needs. What impression will be most reassuring for the participants? How will the plan for the session achieve the goals agreed with learners?

Most online tutors arrive early to set up their session and make sure that everything is ready to go. Having arrived early should the tutor just hang around until everyone arrives? For many tutors, using the 'stepped away' tool to indicate that they are logged in but not available at the moment, allows them to set up the session in advance. They can then return five or ten minutes before the session starts, ready to welcome everyone.

It is helpful to decide what you intend to say as each participant arrives in the room. Good practice involves participants doing an audio check before they are ready to speak, so they appear on the participant list but perhaps need a few moments to get ready. How will you greet them when you feel the time is right? The most frequent opening question is probably to ask each person, 'How are you?' and mostly the replies will be of the, 'I'm fine' variety. This is often the point where people will mention that they have a cold, so please excuse their croaky voice, or that they have to leave early or step away to take a call at some point. To increase the level of participation at this time in the session, it can be helpful to ask everyone to check sound levels by saying something specific, like a comment on what is happening where they are. If this sounds horribly mundane, consider other possibilities – silence on arrival and a prompt start can be quite intimidating for participants. Using a timer and a message on the whiteboard that this is the right place and that the session will start in a certain number of minutes can take away some anxieties. In all cases a parallel conversation in the chat box can help learners to feel welcome, particularly if they are keen to check that the technology is working well.

Deeper topics of conversation may not be appropriate early in a session. Participants may not be ready to open up to the rest of the group, or the topic for the day may need to be introduced and developed before deeper discussion is possible. If participants meet regularly and are known to each other, they may chat directly to one another. Learners may forget that everyone will hear what they are saying, and that conversation cannot be private. If the conversation becomes too personal or exclusive, you may need to become involved in a sensitive way that would be unlikely in a face to face situation.

What your online participants see on the welcome screen in the virtual classroom is also important. Like the dinner table set for guests, this screen is giving an impression about what to expect in the session. It is also an opportunity to provide reminders of materials that will be used in the session or simply a reminder to check audio levels before the session starts. Figure 3.3 shows an example of a simple welcome screen. It includes confirmation of the course and the start time, a reminder of resources needed, a request to set up audio correctly, and information about how to get help if problems arise.

You may prefer a welcome slide which gets individuals involved in something you are going to be working on later in the session. This can be an opportunity to have fun and relax participants as well as to get them thinking about the topic being studied. The example in Figure 3.4 is from a workshop at which learners were considering study skills. One aspect of this topic is the impact of food and drink on the ability to concentrate. By displaying the screen in Figure 3.4 at the opening of the session, it was hoped that learners would begin to formulate ideas about the impact of food and drink on their ability to study before formal discussions started, thus maximising the learning time available during the session.

Figure 3.3 Example of welcome screen

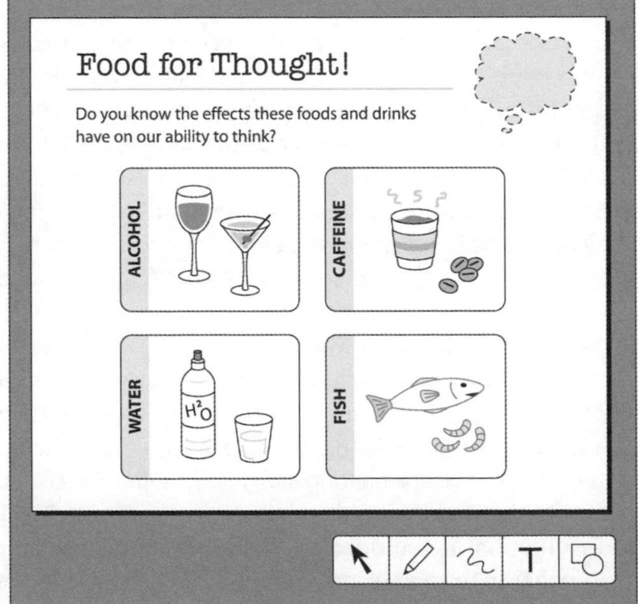

Figure 3.4 Example of pre-workshop activity

Whatever approach is used, the purpose of giving a welcoming first impression is to create a friendly and comfortable learning environment. Perhaps this confirms what has been said already, that using web conferencing for teaching and learning is about making choices that will help learners to feel at ease and facilitate learning by increasing their confidence and their comfort with the virtual learning environment.

▶ Helping learners to connect with one another

It is not always easy to project our personality and make meaningful interpersonal connections in the online environment. The use of web conferencing should, in theory, provide opportunities for participants to make connections with one another, since communication is immediate, and there are a range of media to draw on, including video and audio. Despite these opportunities, research by Ward et al. (2010) suggests that learners may struggle to create their online identity, so facilitators may need to offer support.

Various strategies may help learners to develop connections with other learners, sometimes referred to as creating an online social presence. The following suggestions come from Kleimola and Leppisarri (2008) and Wang and Hsu (2008) and will be developed further in the next chapter:

- the use of personal introductions, so that participants know something about the other people in the group
- discussions of feelings and opinions
- humour
- careful facilitation of interaction
- the development of a sense of belonging.

Video can also be used to enhance social presence, and many facilitators use web cams to give participants the feeling that they have actually met one another. Video from web cams can help participants to communicate emotions and provide information about learners' contexts and personalities. Web cam images reveal what participants look like and sometimes give clues about their social context. The location of learners – at home, in the office, in a coffee shop – or the artwork or books behind them may prompt social chat, further enhancing interaction and a sense of identity. Some tutors find that using video helps to communicate their personality and approach in a way that is not possible when using audio. For example, they may smile as they would in a face to face setting, or use facial expressions to provide feedback and encourage interaction. There are challenges in creating a sense of eye contact using a web cam. It is difficult, for example, to look directly into the camera when you also need to be monitoring what is happening on screen, so working effectively with video may take practice. It should also be remembered that for some learners (and facilitators), presenting themselves using video may also create anxieties and impact on their desire for anonymity, so it needs to be used with sensitivity.

Developing connections with learners online is once again a skilful mix of interpersonal skills and the ability to use the technology effectively. For the facilitator, using these skills is an important part of the process of welcoming learners and giving them the confidence to interact with others in the online environment.

IN SUMMARY

Live online learning sessions bring together mixed groups of individuals who have different levels of technical skills and different ways of learning. In this chapter, we have explored some strategies for making the virtual classroom a welcoming learning environment for all participants.

- **The experience of being an online learner** can be a very positive one if the facilitation of learning takes account of differences in learner needs, expectations and learning experiences.
- **Getting to know online learners** is helped by induction sessions and talking to potential learners before a course starts. When the learners first meet online they may need frequent reminders of how to use the technology and reassurance to build their confidence. Activities which encourage reflective practice on learning skills and habits can be built into online sessions to reveal more about learners.
- **Online learners and technology** go together, so it is essential to make sure that learners can access the technology and use it effectively. Not all learners will be new to web conferencing technology, but in most groups there will be different levels of confidence and skill. Online learners are asked to tackle new information and ideas relating to their course but also to manage complex technology – it is a dual learning experience which can be stressful. It is helpful to offer regular reminders of how to do things and ask participants to acknowledge that they understand what they have to do. If learners seem to lack motivation, involving them in activities that

produce speedy responses, and even rewards, may help to foster a stronger commitment to learning. Feedback can include positive rewards, such as a 'thumbs up' icon, or a round of applause, or simply the approval of the facilitator or others in the group

- **The significance of learner location** should not be underestimated. Our global society means that we can make contact with our learners without specific knowledge of their location. Although access to the virtual classroom may be possible from anywhere in the world that has internet access, different time zones, different cultures and different perceptions of the world can be challenging for the online facilitator to manage. Discussing some of the issues associated with study location with learners can provide a useful topic of conversation and allow you to be helpful in terms of offering support. Knowing about our learners' location means that we can be sensitive to cultural differences and understanding of learners who live or work in different countries.
- **Supporting new online learners** involves providing induction that will enable them to use the technology successfully and confidently. Taking a group photograph, or asking learners to upload individual photographs, can be useful and provide a starting point for the first online session. Asking learners to write down three things they would like their tutor to know about them as they start the course can offer an opportunity for learners to share confidential information and open up possibilities for dialogue with their tutor.
- **Making learners feel welcome online** results from the facilitator's ability to make everyone feel at ease in the virtual classroom. The purpose and plan for an online session should focus on the learners' needs. What impression will be most reassuring for the participants? How will the plan for the session achieve the goals agreed with learners? The welcome can start before the online session. For example, using a timer and a message on the whiteboard that this is the right place and that the session will start in a certain number of minutes can be reassuring for learners.
- **Helping online learners to connect with one another** is not always easy, but there are real benefits for groups of online learners if they are able to interact with one another confidently. The facilitator has a role to play in offering opportunities for learners to share learning experiences.

4 Creating a learning space

So far, we have considered web conferencing technology, the role of the facilitator of online learning and the profile and needs of online learners. This chapter brings the technology, the facilitator and the learners together to consider the importance of:

- creating a virtual space where people can learn
- building trust and rapport
- dialogue, silence and turn taking
- presenting information in the virtual classroom
- learners in conversation with one another.

Creating a virtual space where people can learn

The virtual classroom provides a place for individuals to meet, but how can this be transformed into a learning space? The first step may be to encourage the individuals to feel part of a community of learners, with many of the characteristics of other communities: a sense of belonging, a commitment to the community, and a common goal. The term 'community' is most frequently given to locations where people live, but in fact not everyone who lives in a community has a sense of belonging to their physical locality. Some people who work away from home for most of the day never see their neighbours and feel a greater sense of community with the people they work with. In a neighbourhood, community bonds may only develop when there is a common threat or challenge, such as a new supermarket development or a crime wave in the area.

What is the relevance of these community norms to an online learning community? The most obvious relevance is that a sense of community is not automatic when people are in the same location. People online together may feel no connection at all to the other participants. The facilitator will have to find a way of encouraging participants to buy into the value of a learning community.

Creating an online learning community involves promoting a sense of common purpose. This is often the easiest aspect to build on as those who are taking the course will hope to succeed and will share that hope with other online participants. It is helpful to refer to this common goal regularly, both to improve motivation and to develop awareness that there *is* a common goal. References to assessment or qualifications can be useful as a reminder that everyone will be challenged in the same way by the demands of the course. A shared passion for the subject that is being studied can also create a bond between learners.

Individuals are more likely to feel an attachment to an online group if they can confidently communicate and build connections with other participants. To do this they need to be able to use the technology successfully. However, it is the facilitator who has the key role in helping members of an online group to develop a sense of community and this begins with building trust and rapport within the group.

▶ Building trust and rapport

Although using the technology is a practical skill, using it successfully is also about confidence and feeling at ease. In order to feel at ease, online learners need opportunities to build trust and develop a rapport with the facilitator and others in the group. Believing that trust and rapport are 'good' is the easy bit – finding ways to build trust and rapport online is more difficult. Some learners take a very practical approach to learning, showing no interest in socialising with other learners, instead wanting to get on with the course and achieve their specific goals. Others may find themselves quite unable to interact easily online, missing the cues that come from nonverbal communication. Learners may also contribute far more than is helpful, because there is nothing visible to give them the hint that they should let someone else do the talking.

There are several things that facilitators can do to overcome some of these barriers and build trust and rapport with learners. These include:

- creating a good first impression
- making connections with learners and creating a feel good factor in the virtual classroom
- using language effectively to make learners feel positive about their contributions.

Creating a good first impression

This has already been mentioned in earlier chapters. We began Chapter 1 with an empty virtual classroom and described it as less than inspiring. This is a reminder that learners need inspiration from the very first contact they make with an educational organisation. As soon as learners connect with tutors or trainers they need to feel at ease and to feel inspired. If joining instructions are too complicated, or access is difficult, learners may give up before they even get started. If the tutor or trainer is not welcoming or seems to lack confidence, learners may feel that the course is not for them. These issues apply to face to face classes as well as the virtual learning environment. It is good practice to create a positive first impression – and to present a starting point which mirrors the rest of the course.

Teachers often go to great lengths to make a classroom look more interesting by adding art work or artefacts that are indicative of the subject. This can be an important part of the motivational side of learning, by inspiring learners to achieve the same standards as the work that is displayed. Sometimes the creative approach to the classroom includes fun items, or news articles or inspirational quotations from famous people. The availability of interactive whiteboards in many classrooms has offered the potential for this kind of inspiration to be displayed digitally. An excellent example of this was seen in a course for learning assistants in nursery education. A play house was displayed on the interactive whiteboard with a small child coming out of the door. She appeared to be looking directly at individuals as they entered the classroom and welcoming them. This type of creative approach to beginning a class often provides a positive first impression and is easy to achieve in the virtual classroom.

The tutor or trainer who is ready in the classroom when learners arrive and offers a warm welcome by smiling and greeting individuals makes them feel that they are somewhere that is a good place to be. In the virtual classroom, it is equally important to create this welcoming presence by connecting with learners online.

Connecting with learners

In Chapter 3 we mentioned the value of making contact with new online learners before they start their course, and the importance of warm, welcoming communication at this early stage. In most learning situations, the ongoing relationship with the tutor or trainer is equally important. This relationship is often developed during the interaction that takes place outside the formal learning time, as well as during class time. Opportunities to chat informally or to raise a confidential issue are easier to find in the physical learning environment. Online contact with learners tends to be more public, and informal chat can be stilted. Here is an account from a tutor of a group who used a virtual classroom during a spell of bad weather when students were unable to get to college.

> The first thing I noticed in the virtual classroom was the silence. Several students had logged in and we had checked sound, so I knew they knew how to talk online but they seemed unwilling to chat. This felt very odd as this is a group who talk to one another all the time! Eventually, there were some self conscious comments but it was only when they started to use the chat tool that we found the usual humour that punctuates our sessions together. Coffee time felt weird too, as we all just switched on our 'away' sign and disappeared. There was none of the usual chat or sense of being part of a group who enjoy one another's company. We managed the technology well and all the activities went well, but there was a sense of disconnection. I wondered what this would be like with a group who never meet in person.

To overcome this sense of disconnection the facilitator has to be proactive in helping learners to interact comfortably with others in the group. A good starting point is to get to know the names of participants and something about them. Encouraging them to put a photo beside their name can help, particularly if there are individuals with similar names or something else in common which makes them difficult to tell apart. Using names as part of the process of encouraging learners is usually better than using names to point out problems or to test knowledge randomly. Remembering information about participants can also help to make them feel welcome.

In a physical classroom, the tutor or trainer may get to know individuals by remembering where they sit or something about their appearance. In the virtual classroom, the reminder of a learner's name often comes from the sound of their voice or the memory of something they have said. There is also the advantage of having names listed on a participant list. Most web conferencing systems allow the facilitator to move parts of the screen around. The participant list, for example, can be moved to an area of the screen where all the names are visible without scrolling up and down the list. This ensures that the facilitator can see what is happening to all participants in the group. If they signal that they wish to speak or that they have stepped away or have lost internet connection, the facilitator can clearly see this. It may sound obvious, but it is important to check that each name on the list represents one person. If two students use the same computer, only one name will appear. This is confusing and difficulties arise when allocating individuals to groups.

Using a person's name usually implies that we know them as individuals, and this helps to create a sense of connection. It is also helpful to keep a note of individuals who have contributed or who you have spoken to, so that everyone in the group is given some tutor attention. Creating a record sheet which can be used at each session is a useful approach to the process of remembering who has taken part and also who needs to be encouraged to join in more. Table 4.1 provides an example of this.

Table 4.1 Example of participation monitoring record

Student	Notes	Logged in?	Technical problems?	Participation in small group discussion activity
Student 1		Yes	None	Yes – spokesperson
Student 2	Encourage to take part	Yes	None	Yes
Student 3		Yes	None	Seemed minimal – was absent from group chat – need to monitor
Student 4	May be late		None	Yes
Student 5		Yes	Using laptop and built in speaker – advised to get headset	Yes – some good questions
Student 6		Absent		
Student 7	Disability issues – uses text chat not audio	Yes	None	Yes – spokesperson

The way we offer praise and encouragement can also contribute to the connection we create with learners. Overuse of praise can have the opposite effect. The random use of words like 'brilliant' and 'excellent' devalue their meaning. The most effective feedback is believable, specific and genuine, but this has to be measured against the need to make learners feel comfortable about their contributions and motivate them to continue to contribute. It is very important to help participants to feel positive about joining in, but not patronised by excessive praise. The example in the quote shows how the tutor valued the participant's contribution even though her answer was probably not correct.

> “That's not quite the answer I was expecting, Carina, but it's an important point that we all need to keep in mind.”

Tutors and trainers will also be contributing to the mood of the meeting by the feelings they express. The tutor who says, 'It's good to be here,' is more likely to appeal to learners than the tutor who bemoans the difficulties she has to cope with. Learners are also likely to feel more at ease if their feelings are considered. It can be helpful to give them some choice, for example, consulting them about timing of breaks or the way an activity is organised.

Good humoured comments can help to promote a feel good factor in any classroom, but can also be used as a way of defusing tension, and to avoid alienating learners. In the virtual classroom it can be difficult for the tutor or trainer to gauge the response of participants to humorous comments as there is unlikely to be any obvious appreciation or feedback. When microphones are switched off, an amusing story will be greeted with stony silence even if students are shrieking with laughter at home.

It is difficult to know if the way we behave as facilitators suits our learners and helps to make the connection with them that supports successful learning. It is not always easy to ask participants about this directly, so we may have to depend on reflective practice. It is also possible to make use of the recording facility in web conferencing to play back an online session and evaluate our approach. The quotes provide some reflective comments about this experience.

“I kept saying 'OK' every time I moved onto something else. How annoying for my students!”

“Seeing myself on the webcam was better than I expected, but I did keep looking over the top of my glasses to see the screen. This meant I wasn't looking at the camera and lost eye contact with my group.”

“The session was good but it was very distracting to hear myself laughing so frequently. I spoke and then I laughed, even if what I said was completely unfunny.”

These reflections all suggest that tutors discovered something about their mannerisms or behaviour which they judged to have a negative impact on learners. Helping learners to feel at ease in the virtual classroom involves being aware of potential distractions as well as using positive strategies to create an enjoyable learning experience.

Using language effectively

Communication online should be warm and open. It is important to avoid making assumptions or prejudging learner preferences and abilities. Few tutors or trainers would disagree with these statements, but in practice not everyone chooses language which promotes confidence and reassures learners. For online learners this can be even more important than in a face to face situation as there is no nonverbal communication to soften the words that are used. It is a definite skill to write or speak clearly, and also include enough words to soften the directive nature of any instructions or warnings. Here are some examples.

> Switch on your microphone by pressing the button labelled 'Talk' at the top left of your screen. You can check that you've done this correctly by looking for the microphone icon beside your name in the participant list. (Pause) Well done, I can see a few microphones appearing. Don't breathe too loudly or you won't be able to hear me speak. OK, now switch your microphone off by pressing the 'Talk' button again.

> There are lots of ways that you can get things wrong in this environment so please don't press any buttons until I tell you to. In fact, it's probably better if I do the button pressing and you just pay attention.

> I'm glad to see that you've managed to find your way into our virtual classroom. We're going to start by testing that we can hear one another, so I'll just say hello to each of you and perhaps you could switch on your microphone and reply. It would be nice to know what the weather is like where you are too, so just give me a brief weather report if you can.

The second example is likely to create anxiety, as the focus is on participants getting it wrong and the facilitator taking charge. Along with apologising too much, this is one of the most frequent issues with online facilitation. The facilitator uses language which intimidates learners and takes charge rather than giving learners the opportunity to use the online tools themselves. The other two examples provide clear instructions but also use humour or social chat to give learners guidance on what to do and some idea of what others may hear. Breathing into the microphone is an issue, but giving everyone a warning about it creates anxiety. Similarly, saying 'hello' online can be difficult so giving participants a topic to talk about can be very helpful. This is particularly true if participants are in very different locations, or prefer not to say where they are, but are willing to say that the sun is shining or there is snow on the way.

The connection that learners feel to their tutor or trainer is often affected by the way that tutors or trainers present themselves through their choice of language and use of examples or stories. The example below refers to a very remote online teaching situation with a very large group of students. Here is a comment from a student taking part in a massive open online course.

> I took part in an online history course offered by an American university as part of their online programme. It was an excellent course and I learned a lot. Surprisingly I felt quite connected to the professor who delivered the course. He gave very good lectures in terms of content but it was his style that made the information accessible. Initially he was quite formal but as the weeks went by he relaxed and made occasional references to himself, for example saying he didn't like to read his own books. He spoke about his family once or twice, talking about putting his kids through college. He laughed occasionally with the support team and asked them questions. He seemed approachable online but he also sent weekly emails which had a personal feel to them. He mentioned meeting one of our classmates in the dry cleaners, making me feel that I was part of a group who knew something about one another, even though we were on different continents.

Building trust and rapport between learners and tutors or trainers is a subtle and complex business, particularly in the virtual classroom, but it is achievable and adds significant value to the learning experience.

▶ Dialogue, silence and turn taking

A barrier to building rapport with learners can be the difficulty in having online conversations that feel natural. Web conferencing systems are usually designed to manage participants' input to an online session. The facilitator has privileges which most participants are not given, including the ability to switch off participants' microphones so that they are unable to speak to the group. There is usually an icon which allows participants to indicate that they would like to speak, often allocating them a number so that they 'queue' to make their contribution. The most familiar icon is the hands up sign, which is reminiscent for some participants of school days when they had to ask permission to speak. In a more adult learning environment, dialogue is usually much freer than this and people take turns by observing when there is an opportunity to speak. Sometimes people speak over one another but they are usually quick to apologise and to agree who will speak first. The social conventions of turn taking in conversation are subtle, but familiar. Online these clues are missing and this can lead participants to feel inhibited about speaking, fearing that they will speak at the same time as someone else.

The idea of controlling learner interaction is not usually part of a learner centred teaching strategy. The dilemma for the online facilitator is how to encourage participation but also protect participants from feeling anxious about making contributions. In the early stages of a course it is helpful to explain some of the issues which arise in the virtual classroom. At the most basic level, it is usual to explain that if everyone leaves their microphones switched on there is likely to be interference, so one of the conventions that is usually agreed with participants is that microphones are switched off when individuals are not speaking. This can provide an opportunity to give some information about the ways in which learners can join in. These include:

- using the hands up sign, particularly if they have a question or a problem which the facilitator needs to know about
- using the chat box
- speaking when invited to speak by the facilitator
- taking advantage of a pause in the session and just speaking out as one might in a normal classroom – the facilitator can usually see a microphone symbol beside a participant's name when the microphone is switched on and this can be a sign that someone wants to speak in this spontaneous way. It can be helpful to acknowledge this and invite the participant to speak.

It is helpful to highlight the experiences that learners may have with silence. At the most basic level, it helps to remind learners that it is easy to forget to switch on the microphone, so that the rest of the group hear silence but the participant is speaking. Participants may also like to think about the impact of not being able to speak instantly. This can mean that reflections on a topic are deep and powerful, and worth recording or sharing when the opportunity arises. Our research includes frequent references to the quality of contributions arising from this kind of careful thought, and the powerful insights shared online.

Silence can also become too comfortable! It can become a habit not to speak because it requires some effort. Facilitators need to be aware of this and to find ways of encouraging individuals to contribute. Sometimes it can be helpful to make sure that everyone has spoken at the beginning of the session as this tends to break down the barrier of silence that can become a negative choice. If participants speak at the beginning, they are more likely to speak during the session. Silence can indicate disapproval too or confusion or any number of other negative emotions, so finding ways of encouraging participants to let you know how they are feeling is very helpful. Here is an example of one online tutor's introduction to an activity designed to encourage dialogue in the virtual classroom. Note the similarities with sports commentating, as she keeps a running commentary going to alert the participants to what is happening.

> At the induction session you had a chance to play around with the tools available in the virtual classroom. We're going to begin this session by considering how we can make use of the tools as well as dialogue with one another to increase our sense of what others in the group are thinking and feeling. First of all, enjoy the silence and take a moment to reflect on how we react to silence. Now, type a brief comment into the chat box telling everyone else one thing you thought about silence and learning. (Pause) OK, I can see the comments beginning to appear – someone thinks it's an opportunity, someone else thinks we tend to want to fill silence with some sort of chat, someone else says it's unnerving when no one speaks. Great suggestions, well done! You've covered the issues for online learners very well. It's an environment where we need to be more aware of silence and what it means – yes, it does often mean that the speaker has forgotten to switch on their microphone, but your comments suggest more complex issues. Secondly, I'd like us to consider how we promote discussion online and create a real sense of dialogue. I'd like to use a different technique this time and invite each of you to tell me your preferences when speaking online, for example to be invited to speak or perhaps to use the hands up tool.

This online tutor has decided to deal with the issue of talking online directly. She has also used the opportunity to find out more about how her learners are feeling and something about their preferences. These may change over time: it will probably be useful to revisit this kind of activity later in the life of a course or programme of study. A similar activity, asking learners about learning preferences and challenges, was described by one of the learners.

> We started by practising using the tools. It was quite easy, although a few people made mistakes and pressed the hands up sign instead of the smiley face. It made quite a noise! A number appeared beside each name so no one could avoid being noticed and they were all apologising for pressing the wrong button. I thought the tutor handled it quite well. She said not to apologise for trying out any of the tools. She was just really glad we were participating. Then we did an activity called learning choices. I was getting a bit impatient to get on with the course but actually it was a really useful activity and showed that learning online isn't just about using the tools correctly. We went into breakout rooms in small groups and listed learning preferences and challenges. Then we went back to the main room and collated the lists from all the groups. The tutor was quite skilled at linking our lists with online learning. One student said she preferred to listen rather than talk and the tutor talked about silence online being impossible to interpret and she needed feedback from all learners. I said time to attend workshops was an issue for me and she was sympathetic but went on to talk about the intensity and efficiency of working in a virtual classroom. She called it very good value for money so not to be missed. She did a short lecture after that and I was quite struck by how true her comments about learning were. If we hadn't done the activity on learning I don't think I would have been so aware of what I needed to do as an online learner. It was very intense too, and I was really glad to get a break after an hour and just slow down for a few minutes.

In this example, it seems that the use of breakout rooms has also been helpful for learners, by encouraging participants to meet in smaller groups and share views on a given topic. If the numbers are small it is often possible to leave microphones switched on in the breakout rooms without creating interference and this can lead to a more natural dialogue, without such obvious turn taking when making contributions. Learners often report that they feel more relaxed in the breakout rooms because they are interacting with a smaller number of people and there is less need to signal the desire to speak. Technology can empower learners by providing them with a safe space where they can express their opinions, particularly shy students (McBrien and Jones, 2009).

For some tutors and trainers the process of managing learner interaction can feel uncomfortable, preferring learners to organise their own groups and facilitate interaction themselves. This can happen online, particularly as the sense of an online community grows, but initially, most participants value the support provided by a facilitator in promoting interaction.

▶ Presenting information in the virtual classroom

Most of this chapter has been about building relationships with learners. The presentation of information in live online learning sessions is most effective if it is part of the process of getting learners to interact with one another and with the content of the online session. Presenting information in the virtual classroom requires creativity and imagination if learners are to remain engaged and focused.

At the beginning of an online session, the participants need help with the direction and content of the presentation of information through an agenda or plan for the session. Usually, they can only see one screen at a time and so the facilitator needs to remind them of this agenda or plan and the order in which information is being presented as new screens appear. This includes reminders of what has already been covered and what is still to come. We have already made reference to first impressions and the screen that online learners see when they enter the virtual classroom. This is likely to be the first of several screens that will be changed as the session progresses. The information on each of the screens can support the signposting process, reminding learners where they are in an online session and where they will be going. Figure 4.1 shows sample slides for an online session: these slides would be used at different points in the session to remind participants what stage has been reached.

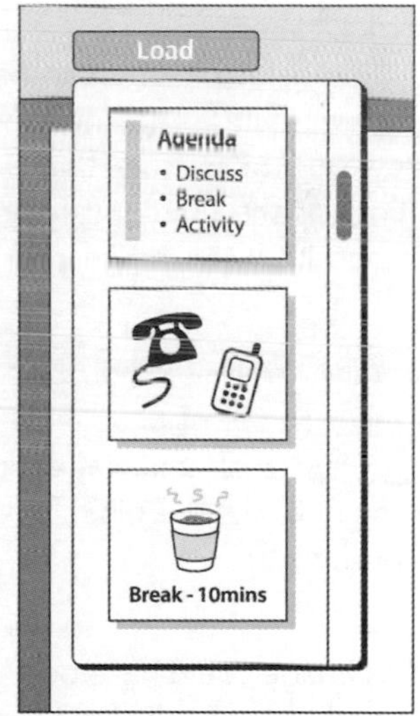

Figure 4.1 Example of presentation slides used to signpost an online session

As the session progresses, participants still need to be reminded of the direction and content of the session. The online facilitator needs to be particularly skilful at keeping the learner in mind and offering support and reminders. Describing what is going to happen and providing pointers about what to look for can make a big difference to learners' confidence. Using tools such as the timer and the system for sending announcements can help this process. Repeating slides may offer an additional reminder of something that has been covered earlier. Using familiar slides to indicate that it is time for a break, or time for questions or a review of the session can also help to signpost progress and activities.

Clear instructions are essential in the virtual classroom. The kind of follow-up instructions after an activity has started that can be given in a physical classroom can be much more difficult in the virtual classroom. A common mistake is for the facilitator to send participants off to breakout rooms before giving instructions for an activity – getting them all back to find out what they have to do is a very clumsy process and can leave everyone feeling a bit disconnected.

Additionally, participants may be less willing to ask questions because it may feel more difficult to ask for clarification online. It is helpful if all instructions are both written and spoken. If instructions are also placed in breakout rooms for small group work, this provides another reminder for participants. It also makes good use of the technology that allows the easy transfer of slides between virtual rooms. Most participants value reminders of how to do things, as well as what they have to do. If learners are asked to type some text on to the screen, they are likely to appreciate a reminder of where to find the text tools and how to change the font and colour of text. Preparing a whiteboard screen that has allocated spaces for each learner may also be appreciated to avoid learners writing on top of one another. It has the additional benefit of giving learners a sense of having their own place in the virtual classroom.

Photos or pictures can be used to share information with learners, helping to create a memory and provide a focus for learning. It is important, however, to be sure that anything visual relates to what is being spoken about at the time and removed when the topic is over. This is particularly important if the image is disturbing, as in the following example.

> I did a criminology course online. Some of the images were distressing, for example of people being hanged, and it was very difficult when the presenter left the images on the screen after he had moved on to the next topic. It made it difficult to concentrate because we could still see these grim pictures.

This image could have been replaced by something less distressing, but also something which helped the participants to track their progress through the session. If there is no visual information to accompany part of the session, it is useful to insert slides which are not a distraction. For example, regular slides could be inserted with a graphic which indicates the type of activity taking place at that point. Participants find it easier to concentrate if this kind of visual clue is provided to help them to find their place in the session. If the same format for slides is used throughout a session, such as bullet point lists, learners find it harder to notice when slides change.

Interacting with text on the whiteboard can help to focus the learners' attention. Specific tools, such as highlighter pens and drawing tools are available in the virtual classroom. Using the pen to handwrite something on the whiteboard can be difficult, producing very shaky, almost childlike writing at times. If this was all that learners could see then it might give a poor impression of the professionalism of the facilitator, but annotating typed text on screen with handwritten comments can create interest and focus attention in a way that typed text alone may fail to do. Similarly, typing a summary on a blank screen as learners express their ideas can be very helpful in clarifying what has been said – and valuing their contribution. The added benefit is that this can be saved for future reference by both learners and facilitator. The amount of information presented on screen also has an impact on learners' ability to assimilate new concepts. Introducing items line by line, rather than presenting a complete screen of information is helpful. Using summary slides frequently can also help.

The learners' imagination can be a valuable learning tool. The online environment can be a very reflective place. The occasional silences, the lack of distraction and the need to signal the desire to speak, can all make learners reflect more carefully on a topic. The virtual classroom offers the opportunity for learners to use their imagination as a learning tool. When the facilitator gives information or shares an idea, learning is only just beginning. Real learning takes place when the learner begins to process the information, relating it to known experiences and beginning to imagine its meaning.

Teaching is a creative process. Experimenting with new ideas that help learners to become more involved with learning material is part of the motivation of many educationalists. This creativity is also part of the excitement of working online – perhaps even more so as there are more challenges online than in a physical classroom, as in the following example.

A nursing tutor wanted students to experience what it was like to be a frail older person, with some loss of memory. In a physical classroom, she would have created a group activity where students took the role of nurse or patient and experienced what it was like to be fed with a spoon, or to be unable to get out of a chair without help. In the virtual classroom, she attempted to create an experiential learning opportunity by asking students to bring along some props: a scarf, a safety pin, a banana and a sealed envelope. She asked everyone to watch the screen for instructions and do whatever they were asked to do. The first screen asked them to make a sling using the scarf and disable one arm. The second slide asked them to try to attach the safety pin to some item of clothing. Then they were asked to try and eat the banana and finally to open the envelope. Here is the tutor's comment on this activity.

> *I was so nervous about trying this. During the activity was the worst time because I had no idea if the students were doing anything, or even if they were still there. I didn't know if they felt offended by being asked to do something that involved play acting. I wasn't even sure if it was going to be a learning experience. All my years of experience in the classroom just slipped away and I felt like a new teacher, completely lacking in confidence. When the final slide signalled the end of the activity, I asked everyone to switch on their microphones. This did create a lot of microphone 'noise' but for once it was worth it to hear the sound of laughter and excited comments about what it had been like to experience disability. In the feedback sheets on the course, it seemed to be the activity that most students remembered.*

Deciding what will be acceptable to adult learners is a common dilemma. It is even more of an issue in the virtual classroom because it is so hard to gauge the reaction of the learners. Perhaps like the tutor in the example, we need to be brave and try things out, particularly if they include fun and an element of gamesmanship which is likely to create a memory and stimulate interest. Here is another example from an online tutor.

I found a web site which created jigsaw puzzles online. I copied a picture of a Christmas scene onto the template and created a jigsaw puzzle. I used it as an opening activity for our Christmas workshop, asking each participant to move a piece of the puzzle into place, until we had a Christmas greeting. It made everyone laugh and the session seemed to start with everyone in a good mood.

These examples of creativity offer some inspiration and a reminder not to be daunted by any apparent limitations of the virtual classroom.

Helping learners to understand and remember information

Presenting information in such a way that it creates a memory or stimulates new ways of thinking is the basis of a student centred approach to learning. Here are some reminders of common ways of presenting information which help learners to understand and remember.

- Most learners remember information if it is presented and repeated in different ways. The virtual classroom offers very good opportunities for this kind of approach.
- Highlighting important information both verbally and visually helps learners. In the virtual classroom this can be done by using a pointer, increasing the size of an item, zooming in on part of a picture or presenting the same thing from a different perspective.
- Providing hooks for learning is important. Starting with something that is familiar to your learners can hook their attention, or something shocking or surprising, or difficult to believe. Asking a question can act as a hook.
- Stories and examples bring a topic to life.
- Pictures, photos and drawings can all help to create a memory.
- Text can also support the words used to present information, but any text on screen should be brief, easy to read and visually appealing.
- Too much spoken information is just as difficult for learners to access as tightly packed text on screen. Allow space for learners to think, by repeating points, asking questions or simply pausing to let ideas develop.
- Signposting content can help listeners if they begin to lose concentration.
- Giving learners something to do, such as taking notes, asking questions or interacting with tools in the virtual classroom, can aid concentration.
- If learners can interact with the presentation, or experience something that is being discussed, or watch someone else in a film clip experiencing what is being discussed, they are more likely to remember the information given.

▶ Learners in conversation with one another

Learners who have chosen an online course which includes synchronous meetings in a virtual classroom have already expressed some kind of choice about working with others. The role of the online facilitator is to make this choice a positive one, by supporting individuals to work effectively online. This may involve selling the idea of collaborative working when introducing activities that involve learners working together. Some learners may feel self conscious when speaking to others in the virtual classroom and this has to be managed carefully. In a physical classroom, the seating arrangement may be designed to promote interaction, for example, arranging seats in a semi-circle. In practice, some people find this intimidating as they feel that they have to talk across the space and sitting facing others makes them feel uneasy. Online, it can feel as if the spaces between learners are infinite and individuals have no idea how to make contact with others.

Overcoming some of these difficulties involves helping learners to feel that they are part of a learning community which values and respects the contributions of others. There are potentially three stages in this process.

The first stage involves establishing a gentle code of conduct which protects individuals and fosters a sense of being part of a group who will work together. There are many strategies in this book which support this approach, but in summary, the facilitator needs to provide opportunities for learners to get to know one another and to interact in a positive way. For instance, as participants are asked to take part in activities during the online session, the facilitator can develop the idea of a code of conduct by giving individuals the right to say 'pass' if they prefer not to answer a question. Similarly, in group activities, participants can be advised to be careful about expressing views that may offend others. In some cases, this gentle approach is not quite enough and a more formal code of practice is required.

Additionally, learners can be encouraged to participate in group discussions. In order to facilitate these discussions it may be necessary to manage difficult behaviour from potential saboteurs. Sometimes the online environment gives individuals a feeling of freedom to express entrenched views. Without eye contact interaction can be different, perhaps individuals feel braver about debating an issue. Keeping a record of who has worked together in small groups helps to make sure that the same people are not in the same group every time. At the beginning of a course choosing discussion topics that are not too controversial or personal is also helpful. Providing support with timing can be important so that everyone takes a turn to speak rather than an individual dominating the discussion.

Offering opportunities for learners to share discussions without the support of a facilitator can also be helpful. Sometimes, students set up their own groups using social media networks, but for some people an online discussion forum which is monitored by an educational institution can feel safer. Some courses encourage students who are near to one another geographically to meet up. It is possible to set up virtual classrooms for use by participants only. This allows them to work collaboratively and use all the web conferencing facilities which support this, such as file sharing and saving records of the discussion. We will say more about this type of activity in later chapters, describing a range of strategies for encouraging learners to work together.

IN SUMMARY

This chapter has focused on ways of making the best use of the technology in the virtual classroom to create a learning space which facilitates communication with and between learners. This is part of the process of building trust and rapport and a sense of online community which supports learning.

- **Creating a virtual space where people can learn** is the goal for online facilitators as they bring together the technology and the people to create a learning community.
- **Building trust and rapport** helps individuals to engage in discussion and learning activities confidently. The facilitator needs to be aware of the need to develop a sense of community in an online group and a shared goal. It is not always easy to build relationships online; specific activities need to be included which encourage learners to share the learning experience and support one another.
- **Dialogue, silence and turn taking** are part of the process of communicating online. This process may feel unnatural for some participants and they may need encouragement from the facilitator to give them confidence to take part in an online session. This can include specific activities which encourage learners to explore their learning preferences and challenges and relate them to the online learning experience.
- **Presenting information** visually as well as verbally helps learners to focus on key points and use their imagination to promote learning.
- **Learners in conversation with one another** explore their views and share ideas with their peers. This may require the facilitator to manage learner interaction and promote positive discussion which involves all members of the group.

5 Engaging learners

Once learners and facilitators are appropriately prepared, live online learning provides opportunities for interaction in a range of ways that would otherwise be challenging or impossible. To support these interactions facilitators need a repertoire of strategies that they can employ to create varied, engaging and effective sessions. This chapter provides examples of activities and strategies that can be used in a virtual classroom. It covers:

- the importance of engaging learners
- introductory activities
- activities that maintain engagement
- effective facilitation strategies.

The importance of engaging learners

Based on personal experiences of facilitating live online learning, Steed (2011) suggests that if you do not engage learners within 20 seconds of logging in they will start multi-tasking. It is very easy for participants to be distracted by emails, an online game or the need to check a web site. Chapter 3 identified the family and office life as other potential distractions. Tutors and trainers need strategies and activities that engage learners quickly and keep them focused. Engaging learners through interaction with content, the technology, other learners and their teachers and tutors can also improve the quality of learning. Researchers have suggested that learner satisfaction and course effectiveness increase as interactions increase (see for example Offir, Lev and Bezalel, 2008; Skylar, 2009).

If participants are welcomed individually, encouraged to introduce themselves and asked about their expectations and aspirations they can be engaged from the very start of a live online session using appropriate introductory activities. These strategies are not uncommon in face to face settings, and can be easily adapted to virtual classrooms. This tutor highlights the importance of early interactions.

> When I meet with a new group of learners my first priority is to get them communicating with each other. I might ask them to introduce themselves

to the person next to them. After an informal chat in pairs, I encourage communication with others in the class, perhaps through an activity that involves them organising themselves into small groups based on particular criteria. Having a bit of fun at this stage relaxes participants and makes conversation easier. We might then create different groups for more substantive activities and the shared engagement in the initial activities provides everyone with something to talk about to help get group interactions off to a good start.

In this example a prerequisite for successful engagement in later activities was effective communication between participants. Encouraging early interaction and communication in a virtual classroom by using appropriate introductory activities will similarly encourage engagement and promote success.

▶ Introductory activities

Chapter 3 demonstrated that introductory activities help learners get to know their peers and help the facilitator get to know them. The examples described used photographs and maps to help establish the identity of participants and supported relationship and community building. Activities that engage learners early in a course or session can have other purposes too. They can be used to:

- **Check learners' prior knowledge** or recall of important information. A simple question and answer approach or an informal multiple choice quiz can reveal information about learners' understanding of key theoretical concepts without it feeling like a test. Polling tools can be used, and summaries created for on screen display.
- **Encourage the development of technical skills**. For example, if learners are going to use drawing and annotation tools later during a session, their confidence with these can be checked or developed during an introductory activity. This will prevent more substantive activities being disrupted by questions about the tools or errors in their use.
- **Help learners focus on being a learner**. Making the switch from the context they were engaged in before the session to being a participant in a learning environment can be difficult. Introductory activities are particularly useful for work based learners, helping them shut out office distractions, focus on course content, reflect on progress and shift their identity from worker to learner.

- **Provide an opportunity for technical problems to be resolved** before substantive engagement is necessary. Unanticipated technical problems can arise when a participant (or the facilitator) joins a session from an unusual location or with unfamiliar equipment. A microphone that has been previously used successfully can develop a fault and need to be exchanged for a backup. Providing 'settling in' time when learners are engaged in an introductory activity means that issues can (hopefully) be sorted out before the core content of the session begins.

However, arguably more important than any of these justifications for using introductory activities is the fact that they encourage early interaction in the virtual classroom, and allow the facilitator to check that everyone can communicate effectively. Effective introductory activities can also be fun, non-threatening and motivating, as the following case study shows.

> At the start of one of the first sessions with a new group, I used a collaborative drawing activity to involve everybody in the class and provide practice in using whiteboard tools, and support for team building. I asked participants to create a drawing of a house on the whiteboard by each contributing one particular feature (see Figure 5.1).
>
> I gave them a time limit of a few minutes. Those who were confident with the drawing tools started immediately, others who were less confident waited. I encouraged people to use the audio to ask each other for help, and allowed several microphones to be switched on at once, so that a relatively normal conversation could take place. I heard someone ask 'Who drew that lovely smoke? How did you do that?' Someone else responded and explained their use of the drawing tools. There was evidence of peer support and collaborative skills development going on. And it was great to hear informal comments and laughter. I hoped the activity gave the impression that this was a friendly and supportive environment where the group could work together, ask questions, get help, and have fun. My role was to create the slide for the activity, set the timer and close the activity with a few encouraging comments about the product and the importance of being able to use the whiteboard effectively. We then used the drawing tools again during an activity later in the session.

The activity above is an example of a team challenge which can be changed to suit different contexts and learner groups. Some suggestions for adaptations, together with details of two other types of activities that can be used

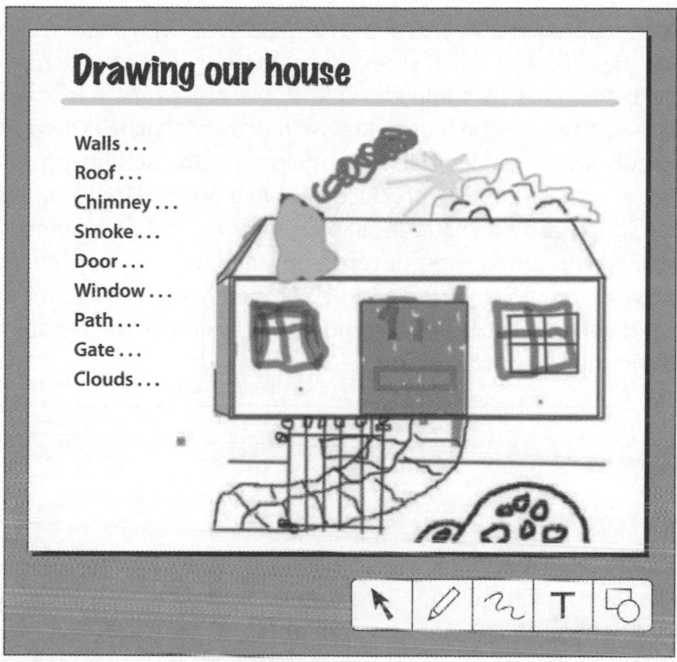

Figure 5.1 The outcome of a collaborative drawing activity. Names of participants were added next to each part of the house.

to encourage early interaction – round table and diagnostic activities – are provided below.

Team activities

Team activities allow participants to work together as one team or in smaller groups to complete a task. The task can be designed for fun and community building, or have a link to course content. One example is the collaborative drawing task outlined above. This could be easily adapted to be more relevant to course content. Learners on a course in geography could be asked to collaboratively complete an unfinished diagram of the hydrological cycle displayed on the whiteboard. Those on a nursing course could be asked to add labels to bones on an image of a skeleton. These activities will generate discussion of course content, support the development of technical skills and allow the facilitator to observe interactions and assess learning.

Another approach uses crosswords and puzzles. With a crossword, one team can be allocated down clues whilst another solves the across clues, and the teams race to complete first. If the crossword has a content-related theme this can be a useful revision activity. Online crossword and puzzle tools are available which can help with the setting up of these activities, and they could be produced as whiteboard slides or in external software which is then made available using application sharing. These team activities promote peer interaction and help develop confidence with software functions. Introducing a competitive element can be motivating and generate a buzz of communication using all the various media available in the virtual classroom.

Round table activities

Round table activities allow each learner in the class to contribute a response to a similar question or prompt. A whiteboard slide could be displayed which shows the beginning of a sentence, for example 'Something interesting I have found on the course web site, read or done since our last session is ...' Learners are asked to raise their hands when they are ready to contribute a response. A time limit can be given to each participant. These activities can be used to help to check technical set up, reinforce protocols for communication and diagnose problems. They are particularly appropriate for smaller groups as they can become time consuming if there are large numbers of participants who each need to be given a chance to respond. Brief feedback from the facilitator is beneficial if time allows.

Diagnostic activities

Diagnostic activities aim specifically to check learners' knowledge or allow their needs to drive subsequent session content. Revision quizzes using the polling tools allow the reporting of responses at a group level rather than focusing on individuals. These can be created with one question per whiteboard slide or prepared in advance using PowerPoint and uploaded during the session. Learners respond to questions using multiple choice response tools, and answers are automatically summarised and displayed on the whiteboard. The relative anonymity of the poll output allows individuals to assess their own progress with reference to the rest of the class, and the facilitator can assess general issues or weaknesses.

An even more straightforward and very learner centred approach to diagnosing learners' needs is to provide a blank whiteboard and allow participants to write up issues about which they have questions to help guide the agenda for a session. Again, relative anonymity is possible, which may encourage open sharing of concerns, and at the same time careful monitoring of the tools being used may reveal where individual weaknesses lie.

Planning introductory activities

Some of the activities above involve interaction with content, and all offer interaction with peers, the tutor and the technology. In all cases it is important that all participants have a chance to contribute, and that the activity is fairly short in relation to the total session time, so that learners do not become disengaged or feel they are waiting too long for the 'real' content to start. Our own research has found that many learners respond favourably to introductory activities used on our courses, and consider them fun, good for putting people at ease, and appropriate for supporting team working. However, there have also been some learners who feel they are irritating and a waste of valuable time (Cornelius and Gordon, 2012). Participation can be encouraged through well designed activities and it may also be helpful if learners appreciate their purpose and role.

Facilitators need sensitivity to learners' feelings and context during introductory activities. This is particularly important during round table activities, to avoid learners feeling that they are being put on the spot. The choices a facilitator makes about questions or topics are important. We found that a learner felt a question which was intended to be friendly and welcoming: 'What did you do during the holidays?' was too personal and intrusive. An appropriate choice of questions or prompts should be given so that there is an option that will suit everyone, and no one is embarrassed or made to feel inadequate. It is useful to give everyone a few minutes thinking time (using the timer), then ask them to raise their hand when they are ready to contribute. In most web conferencing systems this will provide an order for contributions. Those who are more confident, or who just want to get their contribution out of the way, will invariably raise their hand first, whilst those who are unsure have longer to prepare. This also avoids the situation where the person who appears first in the list of participants is repeatedly picked first. Responses are likely to be varied in quantity and quality, so the facilitator needs to be assertive about time management, but also be able to provide appreciative and encouraging feedback. Flexibility is also necessary, for example if a particularly interesting or important point is raised that requires further discussion. Using the responses to guide the content which follows in a session is an example of using the activity in a learner centred way. However, it can be appropriate to keep an activity short and focused, in which case a high level of tutor control may be necessary.

Activities which encourage interaction are particularly important in the early moments of a live online session to help establish a safe and welcoming learning environment in which facilitation can be responsive to learners' needs and characteristics. The next challenge is to keep learners engaged.

▶ Activities that maintain engagement

Skylar (2009: 78) describes the use of questions every three or four minutes during 'web conference lectures' to engage students and encourage interaction. Whilst there could be debate over the optimal frequency of interaction, it is indisputable that frequent interaction throughout a live online session will ensure that learners are engaged and appropriately focused. To sustain engagement during longer sessions, to provide variety across a series of sessions, and to meet the needs of learners, a diverse repertoire of strategies and activities is needed. For newer facilitators these might be explicitly built into session plans, but as confidence grows and familiarity with the software tools develops, it will be possible to introduce opportunities for interaction flexibly and spontaneously in response to learners' needs and feedback. Table 5.1 presents some examples of activities that can be easily adapted to a variety of contexts. In contrast to the introductory activities presented above, there is less emphasis in these examples on interaction with the technology, and more on interaction with content, the tutor and peers.

All of the activities in Table 5.1 can be planned into sessions, and most can be included as and when required in response to how a session is going. If you feel that learners' attention might be wandering, or need reassurance that participants are engaged, then using a quick text question or asking for a response using the emoticons can be very helpful. These activities can also be used to refocus participants' attention when there is a change in topic during a session or to promote engagement with a summary of important points. For example, a set of questions posed at the end of a topic using the polling tools can help the facilitator diagnose participants' understanding of

Table 5.1 Examples of interactive activities for virtual classrooms

Activity	Examples
Quick text questions	Type into the text box some of the subject areas that are taught in your college. What do you think is the average age of a student in your college? Type your answer into the text box.
Collating ideas on the whiteboard	Write on the whiteboard an example of an issue that you face in your own practice. Write on the whiteboard the names of any learning theories you have heard of.
Using a template to collate responses	Pick one of the boxes on the whiteboard. Write your name in it and a question about the topic we've just covered. Write a short quotation from the play on one of the 'post it notes' on the whiteboard.
Using the emoticons (e.g. ticks/crosses, smiley faces)	Please signal with a 'tick' if you have prior experience of working with children. Please show a smiley face if you are happy for me to move on to the next topic, or raise your hand if you still have a question. Let's give John a round of applause for his contribution!
Polling tools (tick/cross, 1,2,3 etc.)	Are you ready to start the activity? Use a tick for 'Yes', or a cross if you need me to go over the instructions again. How many sources do you need to make reference to in your assignment? Vote with A) for up to 2, B) for up to 9, or C) for 10 or more.

content, and it can also help participants identify areas for revision. Where there is a large group of participants the ability to display a summary of poll responses on the whiteboard can be useful to learners and facilitators and avoid the need to scroll up and down the participant list to check for ticks or other individual responses.

Whilst most of the activities in Table 5.1 allow learners to see all of their peers' responses, collating ideas on a whiteboard provides an opportunity for learners to participate with relative anonymity. In most web conferencing software it is not possible to identify who has submitted a particular comment if the whiteboard drawing tools are used. Finkelstein (2006: 100) calls these activities 'magnetic brainstorms' as the ideas can be collected on the whiteboard then moved around like magnets on a fridge door to facilitate organisation and categorisation. A blank whiteboard may be all that is required for these activities, but if more organised contributions are needed (for example to help complete a group analysis of strengths, weaknesses, opportunities and threats for a particular project), it may be helpful to

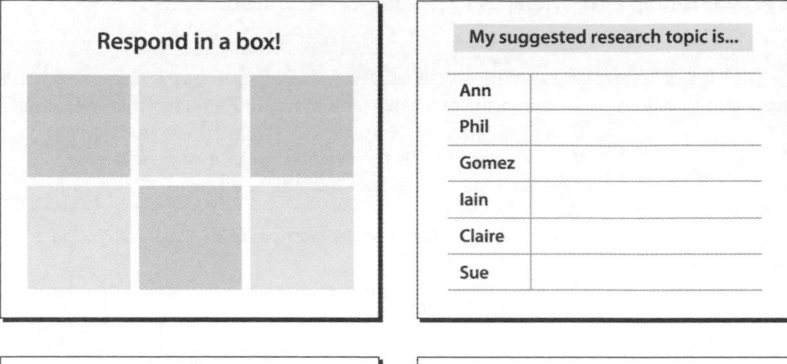

Figure 5.2 Templates for group responses (for a group of six respondents)

prepare a template in advance. Including one space for each participant on a template encourages contributions from everyone. Figure 5.2 provides some examples. Templates like these can be used to gather examples of the challenges participants face in their studies, their suggestions for practices they would like to introduce in their work context, or for a huge variety of other activities. Using the audio tools, participants can be encouraged to say more about their contributions.

Presentation-style activities are not included in Table 5.1 as lengthy monologues do not make best use of the opportunities of web conferencing. However, if presentations are redesigned to include frequent interaction they can work effectively. If content needs to be 'delivered' using a PowerPoint style presentation, a useful strategy is to include slides which break up the presentation with some opportunities for interaction. These could include quick text or poll questions, or other ideas from the list above.

Another strategy which encourages learner engagement and peer to peer interaction is the use of breakout rooms for small group activities. Activities which offer opportunities for collaboration and group work using breakout rooms are discussed further in Chapter 7.

▶ Effective facilitation strategies

Engaging learners in live online learning requires careful planning and management of activities. The main tasks for the facilitator are to ensure that all learners participate, to acknowledge and build on learners' contributions, to monitor interactions, and ensure that appropriate software tools are employed. These tasks are discussed below, along with some of the challenges associated with engaging learners.

In all activities designed to encourage engagement it is important to ensure that all learners are participating. Some of the approaches suggested above identify individual participants, for example, using emoticons or the chat tools. Others allow a degree of anonymity, for instance writing on the whiteboard, and make it difficult to monitor who is participating. Some activities, particularly those which make use of the chat tools, favour those who can type fast. However, all the activities suggested provide an opportunity for everyone to interact and contribute to a session and for these contributions to be acknowledged. It may be too challenging to monitor a quickly developing chat conversation, but it is important for the facilitator to 'notice' and respond to at least some individual contributions. This will help learners to feel that their contributions are valued and worthwhile.

Learners' responses can also be useful prompts to inform discussion and promote deeper engagement. For instance, the question 'What is the average age of a college student?' was posed to a group of lecturers participating in a session, and a range of responses resulted. By scrolling up and down the text chat the facilitator was able to see all the contributions and ask individuals why they had offered a particular answer. In this way further information was obtained about the evidence or assumptions behind participants' answers. Dialogue led to a deeper understanding of the reasons behind the correct answer, as well as an appreciation of the different perspectives that were evident.

Monitoring interactions is also essential to encourage engagement. It can be difficult to remember who has made contributions to an activity or discussion and who has not, and this may lead to a reliance on asking for contributions in alphabetical order or 'from the top down' as presented in the list of participants. This strategy will become tiresome and possibly unfair if overused, and there is always the potential for the list to 'reorganise' itself if participants are unexpectedly disconnected or raise their hands, which can be very confusing for the facilitator. Keeping to hand a written list of participants and adding a check mark against those who have contributed may ensure that you do not ask the same person the same question twice (which will give the impression that you have not been listening), or leave out someone (who may have been keen to offer their opinion or answer). A more overt approach to managing contributions would be to write an 'order of participation' on the whiteboard, checking off people as they contribute. This could be prepared in advance if necessary.

Many strategies that engage learners rely on tools other than audio, particularly text chat, writing on the whiteboard and using the emoticons. These tools provide an apparent equality of opportunity for contribution, but facilitators need to be sensitive to participants' choices and anxieties when they are used. Those who type slowly have already been mentioned, and there will be participants who are reluctant to use particular tools (for example the whiteboard tools), unable to use them due to a physical impairment, or who simply get confused about 'which button to press'. Careful facilitation may be necessary, and as mentioned earlier, strategies to help learners develop confidence with the tools needed for interaction may be necessary. Shepherd, Green and Sampson (2011) outline a strategy that makes the use of the chat tool which is fair for all participants. They suggest the facilitator should pose a question and ask participants to prepare their response in the chat box. Participants are asked to wait to post their response until the facilitator tells them to, so that everyone replies simultaneously. This prevents participants drawing on contributions from others, and everyone is given sufficient time to prepare their answer. Another useful approach is to use just one or two strategies in early sessions with a group (perhaps the chat and a subset of the emoticons available) and then build up the range employed to help learners remain focused on the content of the session rather than the need to remember how to use particular tools. Table 5.2 shows an extract from a lesson plan where this approach has been taken. Only audio and chat tools are required for the introductory activity, with whiteboard tools added later. Careful planning will also prevent disruptions to the flow of the session as a result of requests for help and support with technical issues and prevent interactions with the interface becoming more significant and memorable than engagement with content, other learners or the facilitator.

Facilitators have described their role in a virtual classroom as the 'chair of a meeting', the 'conductor of an orchestra' or a 'ringmaster' (Cornelius, 2013b). These metaphors bring to mind the image of someone working hard to manage interactions and focus learners' attention on what is important. This is a difficult task without eye contact or body language. Adopting the suggestions for effective communication presented in Chapter 4 will help, and there are other strategies that you can use to encourage engagement. These include:

- modelling appropriate interaction
- providing variety
- managing time effectively.

Table 5.2 Extract from a session plan

Time	Activity	What the facilitator needs to do	What the learners will do
09.00–09.15	Welcome and introductory progress check	Explain activity, invite individual contributions, monitor contribution length and provide feedback	Use audio (or chat tool if preferred) to give a brief progress report
09.15–09.20	Purpose and nature of session	Display and explain agenda on whiteboard. Invite questions and feedback using emoticons	Listening. Use chat tool to ask questions, use emoticons to respond to questions
09.20–09.25	Group collation of different literature sources	Display whiteboard slide: *What literature sources have you found useful to support your project?* Explain activity and use of whiteboard tools. Invite individual contributions on the whiteboard.	Write sources on blank whiteboard using drawing tools
09.25–09.45	Discussion of literature sources	Reorganise whiteboard. Invite explanations and probe for further information as necessary. Show preprepared whiteboard slide with list of recommended course literature sources and compare with learner generated list	Discuss contributions and ways of organising information – a confident participant could reorganise whiteboard Listening, contributing, asking questions using audio and chat

Modelling appropriate interaction

All facilitators have experienced the session where it is hard to get participants to engage or contribute. Sometimes there are external or technical reasons for this, sometimes learners may not yet be comfortable in the group setting, and sometimes it can be the facilitator's actions which impede interaction. Overly authoritative facilitators might pose difficult or unclear questions, make judgemental statements about responses or try too hard to pace the discussion, and these actions can have a negative impact on interaction (Duemer et al., 2002, cited in Shi, 2010). Overenthusiastic facilitation, or attempts to take or retain too much control over turn-taking or timings, may be just as ineffective as a lack of control. By acting appropriately themselves, facilitators can encourage effective interaction.

One action that facilitators can take is to use language carefully. In an introductory activity it may be respectful to 'invite' someone to contribute or ask for a volunteer rather than picking on individuals or systematically asking for contributions according to the on screen list of participants. Offering alternative methods for interaction, for example suggesting that responses can be made using either the audio or chat tools, can also be helpful for participants. Where there are second language speakers in a group, the chat tool can be valuable if learners are more confident writing than speaking, and there may be occasions when other learners may not wish to be heard with a croaky voice or for other reasons. A real example is when a learner facing difficult personal issues phoned a facilitator in advance to say that she was feeling rather vulnerable and would join a session but just listen in. Whilst others in the group used audio, she began to contribute using text, and by the end of the session was a prolific and confident participant. Had the session been face to face, she would not have attended and would have missed out on the learning opportunity altogether.

Modelling of the kind of behaviour and interactions you would like to see from your participants is a useful strategy. For example, keeping your own contributions brief may encourage others to do the same. An approach used by one facilitator is to carefully plan timings for his own contributions to ensure that he does not speak for too long. This does require discipline and constant clock watching. However, this facilitator recognised his own tendency to carry on speaking once he had the microphone and the strategy helped him to stop dominating discussions. Learners may also find it hard to stop talking once they get started. A learner who took part in our research reported that she had to 'hold herself back' at times to let others contribute, recognising that she would carry on talking given the opportunity (Cornelius and Gordon, 2012). Learners may need to be encouraged to be succinct – and led by example. If it is possible to have two facilitators present they may be able to model the style of interaction required.

Providing variety

The availability of two facilitators also provides an opportunity for variety in terms of voice and presentation style. Just as two radio presenters may engage in informal chat or use questions to each other to engage an audience, two facilitators can work together to encourage learners to focus during a session. A change of facilitator voice is a useful way to refocus participants when a topic changes or a new activity is introduced by providing a signpost that a session has moved on, or that this is important information to which attention should be paid.

Silences can also provide variety during a session and help participants to catch up and refocus. Short periods of quiet can also be useful thinking and preparation time, allowing participants to focus on a task. Participants preparing answers to questions can be given a couple of minutes of quiet time to prepare their answers, and a timer used to indicate when this is over. During a period of silence the facilitator needs to remain attentive and use other channels, for example the chat, to address situations such as a late arrival to a session.

Another way to provide variety is to use different media simultaneously to engage participants. For example an activity can involve discussion using both audio and chat at the same time. This can be highly stimulating and engaging for participants who are comfortable multi-tasking, but others may find it overwhelming and demotivating. Some facilitators dislike this approach and feel that it creates confusion. McBrien and Jones (2009) suggest that it can be managed by switching off or limiting use of some of the communication channels. A facilitator could choose to disable the chat function for participants, but exerting this level of overt control might be disorientating and even alarming for participants if they are not warned in advance. A better approach might be to try to carefully integrate the two media and explain to participants what is expected from them. This can still be challenging for a single facilitator and may create what has been described as a disjointed 'jerky' conversation in which those using audio can 'push' things and go deeper with their discussion than those using chat (Cornelius, 2013b). However, the two media can be used very effectively together as the following example shows.

> One experience I've had was a large webinar with over a hundred participants. The presenter and a moderator used audio and video. The participants, including me, only had access to chat tools. The presenter asked lots of preprepared questions. He displayed these on the whiteboard screen and used audio to read them out. He asked us to respond in the chat box. The moderator had the unenviable task of trying to summarise the responses as they flashed past on the screen. I was impressed that she did seem to be able to pick out some of the main points and questions posed by participants. I found myself concentrating very hard on the session, but sometimes getting distracted and scrolling up and down the text box to see what others had said rather than listening to the presenter. I would have been interested to know how the contributions from such a large group could be monitored effectively. Could anyone having difficulties be heard? I wouldn't want to work with such a large group, but I could see how the use of two facilitators and different media at the same time could be very effectively used with a smaller group too.

Managing time

Careful management of time is important to participants and will encourage them to engage online. They need to have time to speak and contribute, and they will be more focused if they trust you to finish a session promptly. Not knowing when their turn to contribute will come, and worrying about whether they will need to leave before you have completed the session will create distractions and make it difficult to focus fully on activities and discussions.

Protocols for contributions often focus on using tools such as the 'raised hand' to indicate when you want to speak. This allows the facilitator to call on contributors in turn and ensure that no-one is missed. One facilitator in the study by Cornelius (2013b) talked about this as a fair and democratic approach, and tried to ensure that equal time was allocated to each participant. However, this approach might have an impact on the structure and flow of discussions and can also feel very tutor led and didactic. By the time participant number 10 gets to speak on the original topic the focus may have moved on, so careful management may be needed to keep the discussion focused. Another commonly experienced problem is that participants forget to switch off microphones when they have finished speaking. Gentle reminders are often necessary.

Use of the hand raise tool may not be necessary when smaller groups are involved, since a more natural conversation style can be obtained if all microphones are left on simultaneously. This approach avoids the constant return of the discussion to the facilitator and helps to alleviate the tutor led feel that is obtained if interaction is too tightly managed. Of course more confident participants can be nominated to chair a discussion and this strategy may also help to develop a feeling of learner to learner interaction and control over learning.

In general, it is important to finish online sessions on time. If you do over run you will find that learners begin to drift away to meet other commitments. Better than over running is to deliberately complete a session a few minutes early. This will allow learners to raise any unresolved questions or issues, and provide a valuable informal opportunity to have a chat about progress and problems. Extending an activity until the very last moments of a session will be frustrating for everyone involved and may create a feeling that things are being rushed. This can be stressful for participants and they will become overloaded with information which will not be retained. Setting appropriate ground rules and sharing expectations, as well as ensuring that participants are prepared, will support good time management.

Encouraging and sustaining engagement in a virtual classroom is not always easy, but modelling appropriate behaviour, providing variety and managing time effectively will help. McBrien and Jones (2009: 13) suggest that facilitators should be 'vigilant and proactive regarding student interaction and communication', and the strategies outlined above will actively engage learners in frequent and meaningful interaction.

IN SUMMARY

Learner engagement is critical to the success of live online learning. This chapter has explored the value of engaging learners, outlined strategies and activities that encourage interaction and suggested issues that need to be considered during facilitation.

- **Facilitators should acknowledge the value of engagement** for promoting a quality live online learning experience, particularly the importance of providing frequent and varied opportunities for interaction to keep learners engaged and focused.
- **Introductory activities** can be employed to encourage communication between learners, check technical skills and help learners focus on learning. Explaining the role and purpose of introductory activities will help to ensure engagement.

- **Facilitators should develop a repertoire of strategies** that can be planned or used when required during live online sessions to engage learners regularly and meaningfully. These should be fair and inclusive, and choices about activities should be made with consideration of learners' feelings, needs and contexts
- **Learner centred facilitation** models appropriate online interaction and demonstrates sensitivity to learners' needs and requirements. Monitoring learners' contributions will help with the management of interactions, as will careful time management and appropriate use of language.

Learner engagement is critical to the success of live online learning. If activities that require interaction and engagement are not included in a session, a live event is unnecessary. Instead, learners could be provided with more flexible options for learning such as watching recordings of presentations or exploring relevant web sites. Feedback from learners about whether they are actually engaged during live online learning is important to help monitor success and identify areas for improvement, and Chapter 6 explores issues of obtaining and using feedback from learners in a virtual classroom.

6 Is anybody there?

This chapter is about feedback from online participants and the tools that they can use to let us know that there is actually someone there! We will consider the following issues:

- the purpose of feedback in live online learning
- the duality of the online experience
- using the technology to get feedback from learners
- the role of the facilitator
- different interpretations of learner feedback
- developing the feedback process
- bypassing feedback.

The purpose of feedback in live online learning

The feedback that we get from learners as we work through an online session often develops into a two way feedback process. We are able to gauge student reactions to the learning experience and this in turn 'feeds' our delivery of the session. This is sometimes referred to as reflection in action (Schön, 1987). If students in a physical classroom look bored or are chatting to one another, we may reflect that we need to check that they understand what they have to do, or change our approach to engage all learners in the group. This sort of observational feedback is not always available online, so different ways of evaluating participants' responsiveness to the online learning experience are needed.

One online tutor described delivering a workshop online as 'like teaching with a blindfold on'. It is possible to switch on web cams and microphones, so that web conferencing is more like a face to face class, but in practice this can create distractions for participants. Later in the chapter we will consider some of the feedback mechanisms that are most useful in the online learning environment, but first it is important to consider what use we want to make of learner feedback.

A tutor wrote the following list of objectives for an online workshop.

- Provide an overview of the course assessment
- Reply to any questions
- Check that everyone can use the technology
- Build the learners' confidence in working online
- Build the learners' confidence in working with me!
- Introduce learners to one another to prepare for activities they'll do together
- Make learners feel good about the course and the learning experience
- Introduce humour and variety
- Provide a motivating experience ...

This tutor began her list as most of us do with what she wanted to tell the learners, and what she wanted them to know as a result of the session. As the list progresses, she realises that her purpose is much broader. Perhaps her real priorities are the final items on the list – motivating learners and making them feel good about the learning experience.

Online sessions can have many purposes, particularly when different topics are being presented. It is possible to deliver many of the learning activities that you would include in a physical classroom, so whatever your purpose it is worth trying to find some way of achieving it online. The biggest difference is that the facilitator is unable to see how participants are reacting.

The duality of the learning experience

Adults frequently vote with their feet when they dislike the way a lesson is delivered. In an online session, they can literally switch off or do something else at their desk, and the facilitator is not necessarily going to be aware of this. Most tutors or trainers would agree that engaging learners is one of their primary tasks if learning is to be successful. This engagement usually comes about because the learning experience has been planned with specific learning needs in mind. As the session is delivered there is an ongoing responsiveness to learner feedback, which ensures that students remain involved in the learning process.

The experience of being in a room with students is very different from being together online. The ability of the tutor or trainer to be responsive to the learners in a group is one of the main differences. Compare these two descriptions of the beginning of a lesson in two learning environments, face to face and online.

> I said 'hello' to each of the students as they came into the room but some were so busy chatting they didn't reply. I waited silently for everyone to settle, smiling occasionally if someone caught my eye. One student apologised for arriving late and started a debate in the class about why the buses were being rerouted. I moved to the front of the class and gained eye contact with a few people so that gradually everyone settled and looked at me expectantly. Some had noticed that there was a display at the front of the class of different foods. There was also a model of a body showing the digestive system. I chose to leave admin tasks until later and immediately start engaging them with the topic. I asked everyone to stand and imagine they were eating something and then trace the route of the food through their digestive system. There was a lot of laughter and pointing at one another. When they were seated again I gave them all a hard biscuit to chew and asked them to note the sensations as they chewed the biscuit.

In this example it is very clear that the tutor has used her visual assessment of what is going on in the classroom to inform her decisions about how to start the session. Online everything except the first slide is hidden. Here is the second example which explores how this makes the tutor feel.

> I loaded the PowerPoint presentation and set up breakout rooms well in advance of the online session start time. It's always a worry that there'll be a problem with the technology so the time before a workshop starts is always a tense time for me, and I find it difficult to settle to other tasks. Ten minutes before the session started I put on my headphones and removed the 'away' sign beside my name. The silence can be disconcerting, although sometimes students chat to one another or ask if their sound is fine. It's difficult to know whether to start chatting early and risk making participants feel that they've missed something if they arrive during the chat. At the start time, I greeted everyone and invited each person to say 'hello'. I welcomed them as cheerfully as I could, but as multiple microphones cause noise disturbance, the welcome was very individual and students weren't really greeting one another.

This account of the beginning of an online session has a very different feel to it. A major difference in online workshops is that the tutor has no way of knowing what is happening at the other end of the online experience – is there anybody there? The challenge is to make sure that everything possible is done at the beginning of the session to get participants involved and feeling positive about the learning experience they are about to take part in. Another important aspect of this feedback process is the impact on tutor confidence. If no one is responding to your good humoured comments, you may feel that your learners are not interested, when in reality you are unable to hear or see their responses. This has been described as the duality of the online experience (Gordon, Cornelius and Schyma, 2011).

It can be very difficult to know what participants are doing in practical terms. Perhaps they have been invited to watch a video clip from the internet, but there is no way of knowing if they actually do go and watch it. It is also not possible to tell if participants are actually participating. If someone is quiet, does that mean they are listening and thinking about the content of the workshop or does it mean that they are texting a friend? In a physical classroom setting they may also be sending a text, but there is a chance that you would see this and hopefully try to find some way to get their attention again. Perhaps we also have to ask whether it matters if participants text a friend, write a shopping list or phone a colleague during an online session. In our multi-tasking world, perhaps it is the norm to do more than one thing at once, including studying. An online example of this is found in webinars that have a simultaneous chat stream in order to open the session out to a bigger audience.

The distinction between being on-task or off-task during a workshop is an important one. Many learners are more focused when they are online. Many online learners are also more focused on what they want to get from a learning session and will pick selectively from the content, so that their time is used in the most productive way. Consider the following two examples and whether the tutor or trainer in each case should be worrying about what the students are doing.

> Just before the online session the mail was delivered and I was really pleased to get a favourite catalogue. I took it to my desk with my coffee and logged onto the session as usual. There was a bit of participation at the beginning, ticking boxes to say we were there and giving a thumbs up sign if we could hear OK. The tutor then went into his presentation. I don't like the sound of his voice very much (I think *he* really likes the

sound of his voice!) so I turned down the sound a bit and prepared to listen. The first few slides were fine but then he went over something I knew, so I had some coffee and opened my mail. The temptation was too great! I started looking at the catalogue and lost the flow of the presentation.

In this case, the learner lost motivation because of the style of delivery and the low level of learner participation required by the tutor. She had also adapted her behaviour to cope with an aspect of the delivery that she disliked, turning down the volume to avoid the sound of the tutor's voice. The following example also includes the issue of distractions, but with a more positive outcome.

My colleague and I both take the same course online and do the workshops together in our shared office. At first it felt a bit weird to be sitting in the same room and talking to one another online using headphones. Because we know one another very well, we've become the jokers in our group, trying to get others on board and having a bit of a laugh. The tutor is really up for this and leaves a bit of space for chat about the weather or football. He goes round the group asking everyone to speak, so it's not just us, but we seem to be more relaxed with one another and that helps others to be friendly. Even though we're in the same room, we do use the chat tool to send messages to one another, sometimes asking about the content or what we should do next, but sometimes just checking when the next break will be. The tutor can read our messages – he told us that at the beginning – but he seems to find it useful to know what we're thinking and will sometimes ask if he can share our message with the whole group and give an answer to everyone.

In this case, the tutor has obviously made some decisions about how to make use of feedback from members of the group, and also how to use the situation of colleagues in the same room. It might be tempting to tell them to ignore one another and focus on the workshop, but this tutor has wisely capitalised on their good humour and desire to interact with one another and others in the group.

The online facilitator has to be aware that online learners may be multitasking and open to distractions and disturbances. This awareness can then lead to positive uses of strategies to keep learners involved and to make use of known distractors – invite your participant to introduce their dog to the rest of the group, if that's what it takes!

▶ Using the technology to get feedback from learners

Making things happen online can be a challenge. The facilitator needs to be technically skilled, in order to use the available tools successfully, but also needs excellent interpersonal skills to support and encourage learners to take part in online workshops and to give feedback on progress. The tools are the easy bit. Web conferencing systems offer a range of tools to gain feedback from participants. If the facilitator ignores these tools, a valuable opportunity for getting learner feedback is lost. Participants will also use them successfully if they are given frequent reminders of their value.

The chat tool

The chat tool has many uses, particularly for informal chat, queries and as a substitute for sound if problems arise. These have been mentioned in earlier chapters. It also has the potential to create a distraction, like whispering in a normal classroom setting. Because it is often used informally, it may be overlooked when considering ways of interacting with learners and its potential as a learning tool. We have already made reference to the use of the whiteboard as a tool for participants to type answers that everyone can see. If the question they have to answer requires information on screen for them to review, they can type answers into the chat box without losing sight of the screen. Participants may be able to type text more easily in the chat box than on the screen. Participants can save both the contents of the chat box and the whiteboard – or the facilitator can place them in a shared area for easy access for everyone.

In the example which follows, participants were shown various models of reflective practice and asked to comment on them in the chat box. The models were left on the screen for reference. It can also be helpful to explore your own experience of using the chat box. One of the tutors we quoted earlier found it a useful starting point for making contributions. The case study below provides a completely different perspective which says something important about the opportunities and challenges of the live online learning environment.

CHAT

Learner 1: I like the idea of reflection with peers. I have kept a journal but found it became quite negative. In contrast, a chat with a colleague gave me a bit of a boost.

Learner 2: The theory with the four lenses works for me. Instead of just thinking about what I feel, I try to see things from other people's perspective. It also reminds me how easy it is to base my teaching plans on my own learning experiences.

Learner 3: The 'in action, after action' thing makes most sense to me.

Learner 4: Sorry to be negative but I find the whole thing very self indulgent. There's a job to be done and it doesn't matter what I think or feel we just have to get on with it.

The chat box drove me mad the first time I took part in an online seminar. It was so rude and intrusive. The poor presenter was trying to keep us focused on the topic and all these messages kept coming up. People wanting to be heard instead of listening! Well, I said all this to a colleague and she kindly pointed out that I had obviously been educated in the dark ages when talking in class was discouraged. Suitably chastened and embarrassed – I vowed to be more open minded next time. Amazingly, what I discovered was that the chat box provided another dimension for thinking – almost as if information was received from the tutor, processed on one level by me, then reviewed on another level, as I read comments in the chat box. By the time I did my third seminar I was really beginning to manage to process all the different strands at the same time, but the real breakthrough came when I did a seminar with a tutor who gave instructions to help us make best use of the chat strand for a specific activity.

Emoticons

Another useful feedback resource is the selection of icons called emoticons. As the name suggests these icons are used to indicate our emotional response to what is happening online. Emoticons such as those shown in Figure 6.1 are commonly available.

Figure 6.1 Examples of emoticons

Like so many of the tools and resources available in web conferencing systems, participants use them successfully if they are given frequent reminders of their usefulness. If online facilitators introduce the emoticons in the first online session but then never mention them again, it is unlikely that participants will make good use of them. At different stages in a workshop the facilitator can encourage participants to join in by choosing an emoticon that shows how they feel. The more frequently this is done, the more likely it is that participants will use them spontaneously to give an indication of how they are feeling without being asked. The following suggestions for the use of emoticons are included in a lesson plan for an online workshop.

- 09.30 welcome + invite all to choose an emoticon to show how they feel this morning.
- 10.00 learner group work feedback + use applause icon as each group makes key point, praise anyone who gives other learners applause
- 10.45 after break ask learners to use emoticons to indicate comfort level with workshop content so far. If responses are positive test learning with quiz, if negative, ask for more detail of difficult topics
- 11.15 review course assessment and ask learners to interrupt frequently with emoticons to show how they feel
- 12.15 end of workshop, hope that learners will give me a round of applause!

The aim is to get participants to link a feeling with an emoticon on their screen and use it to express that feeling as often as they wish. This use of emoticons can provide a form of nonverbal communication that is even more powerful and affirming than facial expressions in a normal classroom setting.

A similar way of getting feedback is the use of symbols or pictures taken from Clip Art. Again, participants do best if they are invited to use the symbols regularly. By placing a symbol on the whiteboard, participants can comment on how they feel. In the sample lesson plan, some of the emoticons could have been replaced with symbols.

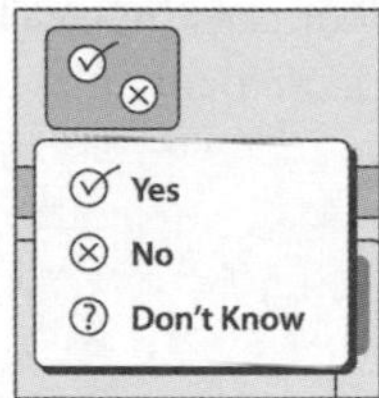

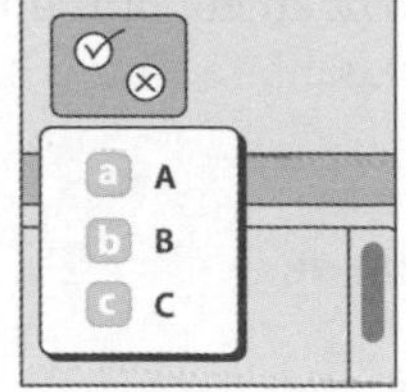

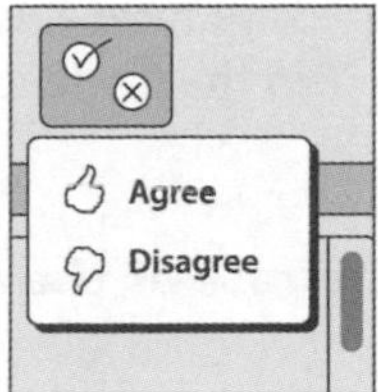

Figure 6.2 Examples of voting tools

The voting tools

Another useful method of getting feedback is the use of voting tools such as those shown in Figure 6.2. There is usually an option to vote for a particular answer to a question, and statistics for responses can be displayed.

Voting tools can be used to get feedback on how useful all or part of a workshop was for participants, but voting may provide quite a superficial evaluation when used in this way. Associated with this is the simple voting tool, which allows participants to give a tick or a cross which appears beside their name in the participant list. Most online tutors and trainers make use of this to check that everyone knows what to do, or has received information, or carried out a particular task – it also checks if participants are there and awake!

It is a very useful tool, but, like so many useful tools, it requires thoughtful management and planning to avoid alienating learners. The tick and cross is best used to indicate that students are able to do something. However, asking everyone to tick their name on the participant list if they understand what you are saying may generate a list of ticks, followed later by evidence that individuals had missed key points, as is illustrated in Figure 6.3. Many tutors regard this as a significant challenge online. Asking about comprehension using this method can lead to feelings of exposure if only one person is honest enough to put a cross against their name.

Figure 6.3 Example of participant list with ticks and one cross

We suggested earlier that the use of these tools is the easy bit. Facilitators need to be technically skilled in order to use the available tools successfully. They also need the skills to support and encourage learners to give feedback on progress. Perhaps the examples we have already provided confirm this. So what can the facilitator do to help the feedback process?

▶ The role of the facilitator

Getting feedback online depends on the tools we have described so far, and also on the management of the online session by the facilitator. Some aspects of this depend on skills we have already discussed, such as building rapport with individuals and the group, but there are some issues that are specific to the discussion of feedback online.

Firstly, the place of feedback in the scheme for an online session is important. When planning a workshop it is important to plan the use of feedback and to be aware of the ways in which it is different online and in a face to face situation. Secondly, the use of language is important. Without nonverbal cues to support language, we have to choose our words more carefully, particularly when we want participants to answer a question or give feedback on their progress. Thirdly, our responsiveness to the behaviour of our learners is important. We need to make them feel valued and involved.

From the learners' perspective, the use of language and the encouragement to offer feedback is important. Consider the following dialogue and the clues that are being given here by different participants.

Tutor: Is everyone feeling OK about the assignment now?

No response

Tutor: Could I ask you all to give me a green tick if you feel OK about the assignment task that we've just discussed.

Slowly, but unconvincingly ticks appear beside all names except one.

Tutor [*sounds relieved to have something to work on*]: I see you haven't given me a tick, Jim. Do you have any questions about the work you have to do?

Jim [*slow to reply*]: Well, I'm not sure. Perhaps we won't really know if we're OK until we get started on the assignment.

Tutor: Yes, I see what you mean. Let's try another approach. In the text box, give me a mark out of ten for your comfort level with the assignment task. Ten means that you're very comfortable, zero means that you're not at all sure what you're being asked to do.

Marks out of ten slowly appear, but four participants don't take part.

Tutor: I see that most of you are giving me a six or seven. That seems OK, but what about those of you who haven't given me a mark?

Again, there is silence and the tutor then asks a participant who didn't give a mark what she thinks about the assignment.

Stella: Actually, I feel the same way as Jim. I don't know what I think until I get to work on it.

Her irritation at being asked the question unnerves the tutor a bit and he rushes on to the next person who didn't give a mark.

Jo: I don't agree with what we're being asked to do. I've already got a masters degree in another subject and we didn't have to do all this stuff that you're asking for.

Tutor: Yes, well it's not me who's asking for it, the university sets the criteria for all assignments at this level.

The tutor's defensiveness leads to a further silence, until one participant tries to move things on.

Andy: I wonder if we could just go over the arrangements for getting help with the assignment once we get started on it.

The tutor has made determined efforts to get feedback from his learners, so why does he seem to alienate his students? Perhaps the fundamental flaw here is that the approach to getting feedback used by this tutor would be commonly used in a physical classroom, where the nonverbal feedback from the group would help the tutor to gauge their mood.

In this case, the tutor might have done better to plan for individual meetings at another time so that participants had time to consider the assignment. Any antagonism could focus on the individual's needs and remain private. The tutor here opened with a general question and when there was no reply, he tried using the tools available in his web conferencing system. This led to the kind of exposure for individuals that we have already discussed. He ignored the potential feedback which suggested that individual participants preferred not to commit themselves to an opinion. The irritation they expressed at being asked publicly to account for their lack of participation suggests that the tutor had ignored the feedback in their silence. Of course, sometimes, silence in a situation like this is a request for attention. Participants who prefer not to be questioned are more likely to give the expected answer, or the same answer as others, in order not to attract attention to themselves.

A different and more positive approach to feedback is evidenced in the following case study.

Tutor: I'd like to try something a bit different in this workshop. It's helpful for me to know how you're feeling about the work of the course, but it's not always easy online to gauge your responses. In the following activity, I'm going to ask you to fill in the answers to some questions on the screen. Your replies will be anonymous, but if you want to say more later then feel free to claim your comment and add to it in person. On the next screen, you'll see a question asking you to identify the part of the course that you feel OK about. There are boxes for each of you and the number I sent you before the workshop by email indicates which box is yours. If I get a completely blank screen then we'll move swiftly on to the next question which asks you to identify the part of the course that you feel most worried about.

There is a pause while participants write on the screen.

Which aspects of the course do you feel OK about?	
6. I like the reading material and feel that I'm learning a lot from the journal articles.	9. *The practical part of the course work is where I feel most confident. It's really my daily work and so more my comfort zone.*
4. Writing essays scares me so I've been pleasantly surprised that I'm enjoying the e-portfolio work so much	2. **No comment!!!**
8. The technology was my biggest fear, so I'm amazed to be saying that I'm really enjoying the different uses of technology. The induction day helped a lot – and my young nephew keeps me right!	7. I take the course text book on the train to work every day and I'm pleased to be getting through it by reading a few pages every journey.

10. The reading	1. Things have been difficult for me health wise and I feel very behind with all parts of the course, so sorry I don't feel OK about anything.
3. I'm last writing my comment so can just agree with 6 and 4.	5. I'm more confident with everything than I expected, but still worry a lot about finding time for the course work and I still worry about failing.

Tutor: Well, no blank screen that's a relief! Thank you all very much for your comments. They're very encouraging for me and it's reassuring to know that some of you feel OK about different aspects of the course. It's interesting that you mention how you felt about some things earlier in the course and how things have moved on. Is there anything anyone wants to add or comment on? Take a couple of minutes to read what's been said and then use the hands up tool to let me know that you'd like to say something.

The tutor uses the timer to give everyone an indication of how long they've got to think about making a comment. This also makes sure that the tutor's impatience to keep things moving doesn't override the need to give participants time to reach a state of readiness to speak.

Tutor: We've got four hands up. Does anyone else want to add to that? Let's start with the first hand, Susie.

Susie: It's not really a comment on the course, but I wanted to say how much I feel for the person who has been ill. That happened to me in the last module we did and it was awful. I'd be happy to help whoever it is – no need to say just now, but do email me if you'd like a buddy who knows what it's like to get seriously behind!

Tutor: That's a kind offer of help and good to let someone else in the group know that you got through a difficult time and you're still on the course. Andy you're next.

Andy: I'm not enjoying the e-portfolio as much as I thought I would. I'd almost prefer an essay, you know, get it over in one go. The portfolio is always there, with another task waiting to be done.

Tutor: That sounds like something we should discuss in more detail and try to work out why two members of the group are finding the experience so different. Thanks for raising that Andy – it's good to have different opinions, so hopefully others in the group will feel encouraged to give their views.

Roger: I'm the 'no comment' person but now I've read everyone else's stuff I think I do want to say that it's really helpful to know how others are getting on. I'm not really a fan of learning online but there isn't a local course that I can do. I miss the chat with other students and sometimes feel I'm the only one who's struggling.

You may feel that this tutor is being overly caring and too encouraging, but the online facilitator role may not always feel natural and there are risks associated with having too much 'bite' in your online commentary. What this tutor did seem to achieve was a greater openness from participants than the previous tutor. He certainly got some useful feedback and learners made connections with one another, which seemed likely to be helpful. The elements of this feedback session that seemed to work online were:

- introducing the request for feedback in an open way and acknowledging that tutors depend on the honesty of learner feedback
- providing time for learners to gather their thoughts and prepare what they want to say, but making initial contributions anonymous – giving individuals a numbered space on screen can also make them feel more comfortable about contributing
- allowing individuals to choose to speak so that no one was asked to comment on what they had said, or not said
- valuing other participants picking up on issues rather than the tutor
- appreciating contributions and welcoming debate
- offering opportunities for further discussion of important issues that were identified by participants.

Different interpretations of learner feedback

It is possible to take feedback personally, believing that learners' comments are about our competence or our approach. Sometimes this is true and there is a need to review our strategies and try to meet learners' needs in a different way. Often, however, their feedback is not directed at the tutor but gives an indication of their needs. The difficulty for many of us is to really hear what is being said and not make assumptions based on past experiences or our own fears or insecurity.

An important skill for online facilitators is to take time to consider responses online and consider what specific feedback means, without making assumptions or prejudging the content or the person. It also allows time to find out more about what learners are feeling and experiencing. It gives an opportunity to keep learners in step with what is happening in the course, rather than allowing them to fall behind or become frustrated. The tutor or trainer needs to get into the learners' shoes and walk around with them for a while before responding to feedback. It is also important to keep in mind that individuals react in different ways and their reactions mean different things. Three different learners are considered in the following case study, each one reacting to the same situation in a different way, and all failing to reveal how they really feel.

Tutor: Apologies everyone, but we'll need to change the time of our next meeting. I can't make the evening time that we arranged before, so could we make it 3.30 instead? How does that suit you?

No reply.

Tutor: Could you give me a tick if you agree with that time?

Four out of seven participants give a tick, agreeing with the change of time.

CHAT

Learner 1 to learner 2: That's ridiculous. I can't leave work early to go online.

Learner 2 to learner 1: I can't make it either. He gave us the dates and times and he should stick to what he said.

Learner 3: The earlier time isn't possible for me, but you go ahead and perhaps I could get a recording of the session.

By changing the language and the approach, a different tutor with the same issue gets different feedback.

Tutor: We should be meeting online next Thursday evening, but I have to have minor surgery earlier in the day and won't be able to drive to work. I probably won't be much fun either. How do you feel about changing the arrangements? I know that you've had this date in your diary for some time and some of you will have difficulty making any other time, so I thought you might like to go into breakout rooms and speak among yourselves about what would suit you best. Perhaps the same groups as last time could go into breakout rooms and then list your comments on the whiteboard and I'll copy them into the main room when we come back together. I know you won't want to take too long over this, so let's say five minutes chatting and five minutes back in the main room making a decision about what to do.

The groups report back.

Group 1: We would prefer to cancel the meeting altogether. There are different issues for the three of us, work, childcare etc which mean that we can't commit to another time. We wondered if you could send us something to work on that would replace the workshop.

Group 2: We quite fancied meeting without you – it gives us a chance to chat and we can do some of the activities if you load them up beforehand. Didn't you give us moderator privileges once before so that we could take charge?

Group 3: We got a bit side-tracked talking about how much pressure we feel under to complete the next assignment, with work and everything else. We didn't actually get round to writing ideas on the whiteboard but the suggestions from the other two groups might suit us all. Those who would prefer to cancel can work alone, and those who want to meet can get together online.

It is not always this easy to resolve issues as a group, but both case studies tell us something about use of language and approach when dealing with adult learners who have busy lives and may find learning online is another pressure. In the first case study, the tutor gave no explanation for the change of plan, failed to apologise, or acknowledge the impact on learners. He used the words 'we'll need to' whereas the second tutor began by asking 'how do you feel about'. Giving learners the opportunity to discuss the issue openly avoided the negativity of the chat box comments and allowed the learners to formulate a solution that suited them. The second tutor was open to feedback from the beginning and as a result gained valuable information about the learners' circumstances and worries.

An effective feedback process is integral to the whole learning experience. Choosing words carefully and being sensitive to learner needs is an important part of this process, but it is also important to develop feedback strategies which are an integral part of the learning process and become familiar to learners.

▶ How can we develop the feedback process?

To develop the feedback process, we need to keep it on our agenda, including it in lesson plans and developing learners' online skills in giving feedback. As the relationship with learners develops, hopefully they will become more confident about giving honest feedback and enjoy debate and dialogue which values different perspectives. It can also be helpful to explore experiences of giving and receiving feedback online. It is useful for tutors and trainers to be online participants themselves, discovering why the feedback strategies they experience are useful or not. This helps to develop models of good practice and new approaches based on personal online learning experiences. Here are some accounts from online tutors who recorded some of the things they experienced online and how it affected them as tutors and as participants.

> “The lack of feedback created real challenges for participants. For example, without any indication that someone had left the virtual classroom participants felt as if they were talking 'to a wall' or 'into the ether'.”

> “The facilitator was very good at waiting for learners to complete what they had to say. This seemed to allow them to deepen their contributions without disruption.”

> “There were some benefits resulting from the feedback tools available. Participants reported that they occasionally received applause – something that was unusual in a face to face classroom.”

> “Gesture and body language are hard to interpret when the web cams are on. Participants don't always look directly into the web cam, so eye contact is different. Sometimes it seemed easier to hear feedback when the speaker wasn't visible.”

> “The facilitator used clues provided by the software to let participants know that their situation was noted, for example, if anyone was losing their internet connection. He also noted if microphones were left on and if anyone was preparing a chat message.”

Feedback is also part of the general interaction that takes place between learners and facilitators. Developing interaction online almost always improves the feedback process. It is helpful to look for ways to maximise opportunities for making connections with learners. This begins before the session starts, during the first moments of any online session and as the session develops and comes to a close. A lesson plan for an online session should reflect the need for learner participation at all stages of the process, rather than phases when tutors deliver presentations and students are silent, followed by phases when students discuss topics with one another. The following pointers are all designed to help in the development of feedback strategies.

- Choose content which promotes interaction. Include questions, ask for examples from the participants and link the content with what is familiar to them.
- Vary the online approach, keeping the participants in mind. What do they need? What are they feeling and experiencing? Perhaps an activity could involve small groups rather than individuals, or maybe a break is needed earlier than planned.
- Introduce hooks to capture interest as often as possible. For example, if someone is buying a house, suddenly everyone seems to be buying a house too, but actually, they are just being hooked by conversations that relate to something that is important to them. Online we need similar hooks to catch the interest of participants, just at the point where interest might begin to wane. The word ‘assessment’ can often have this effect!
- At any point in the process it can be helpful to hand over to the participants, not as a way of opting out, but as a way of involving them. Participants can lead a discussion or tell a story, but they can also carry out practical tasks such as loading a slide they have prepared or sharing a file, or accessing the internet.

The web conferencing tools combined with your online presence promote interaction and help to develop the feedback process. The warmth of your online voice and your use of language can make a big difference to learners. Showing empathy and appreciation regularly helps learners to feel that they contribute to the learning of the whole group.

▶ Is there a case for bypassing feedback?

Perhaps, the expected answer to this question is 'no', given all that has been said about responsiveness to online learners, but the answer is almost certainly, 'yes'. The online facilitator has a position of power, granted to him or her as part of the role. Most participants regard this position as valuable and expect the facilitator to take charge. In fact, they can become quite frustrated if the facilitator fails to take charge and allows abuse of their learning time.

Web conferencing offers opportunities for so much more than passive listening: it also allows the participants to take over and voice personal issues that may not be appropriate or detract from the learning experience of others in the group. If someone in the group has a grievance of some sort it may be necessary to decide that in the interests of other learners this individual will have to be ignored or diverted – as sensitively as possible. It is helpful to develop a selection of phrases that are useful in difficult situations. These types of responses are probably familiar to most tutors and trainers, but online there is an additional difficulty in appeasing or managing a difficult interaction with a learner. All the power is in your words and your tone of voice. There is a real skill in moving things on so that learning is the priority.

Online learners are likely to have different levels of skill, different ways of learning, and different issues in their lives. In a physical classroom these differences are often difficult to manage, but online the tutor or trainer is further disadvantaged because it is not possible to see learners and gauge their reaction to the learning experience. There are fewer informal opportunities to chat to them individually, or to pick up clues in coffee breaks for example, about how they are feeling. What can be even more frustrating is that they are often not willing to speak out about how they feel. To maximise learning and minimise the need to manage individual behaviour, feedback strategies need to be a key part of live online learning sessions.

IN SUMMARY

- The purpose of online feedback is to build rapport with learners and get helpful feedback which may identify their learning needs. The visual clues that are helpful in a physical classroom are often missing in a virtual learning space.
- The duality of the online experience means that facilitators and learners may not share the same experience online. The importance of participant feedback is to try to limit this duality and create a

genuinely shared experience. The online facilitator has to be aware that online learners may be multi-tasking and open to distractions and disturbances.

- Using the technology to get feedback from learners helps to involve participants as well as getting information about their learning experience. Facilitators should use appropriate web conferencing tools regularly and encourage participants to do the same. If tools are introduced at the beginning and then not used again, it is likely that participants will forget that these tools offer a valuable way of communicating online.
- The role of the facilitator is to value contributions from learners and welcome debate and feedback which help in understanding the online learner's experience. The facilitator is most likely to be successful in getting feedback if language is used sensitively and individuals are given choices about how to contribute.
- Different interpretations of learner feedback may lead to misunderstandings. It is easy to assume that a learner is dissatisfied with some aspect of a course, when in fact the concerns are more personal. The online facilitator should be aware of this and take time to work out the real meaning of feedback.
- Developing the feedback process is about including feedback strategies when preparing online sessions. A lesson plan for an online session should reflect the need for learner participation at all stages of the process, rather than phases when tutors deliver presentations and students are silent, then phases when students discuss topics with one another. It is also important to experience the role of live online learner and reflect on how it feels to be a learner and give feedback using different strategies.
- Bypassing feedback may sometimes be necessary, but the successful use of a range of feedback strategies can help to minimise difficult situations created by individual contributions.
- Feedback from learners should be an integral part of online learning, creating a comfortable cycle of listening, responding, valuing and learning.

7 Learners working together

This chapter focuses on the design and facilitation of group work activities which support collaboration and co-creation during live online learning. Examples of activities which make use of breakout rooms are provided, and issues that need to be considered during facilitation are discussed. Some of the issues covered in other chapters, including obtaining feedback, monitoring learner activity and assessment, are reconsidered here in the context of group work. The chapter covers:

- the role of collaboration and group work in live online learning
- preparing for group work
- effective group activities
- facilitating group activities
- learner led group work.

The role of group work in live online learning

Some facilitators new to live online learning rely on whole group tutor led approaches and seem initially reluctant to use breakout rooms in which small groups can work independently. However, small group activities provide opportunities for discussion and co-creation that are known to be beneficial for learning. Since most face to face group work strategies can be adapted for a virtual classroom, activities that support learners working together can easily be part a repertoire of strategies for live online learning. And in many examples of innovative and effective practice using web conferencing it is collaborative activities, often using breakout room tools that form the core of sessions, rather than tutor led presentations.

Another reason to explore group activities is that many learners value opportunities to work with peers. They enjoy well designed group activities and find them beneficial for their learning. Students on our courses frequently cite the opportunity to discuss issues with peers as a key benefit of their experiences. They particularly value:

- activities that require them to work with people they would not normally meet – these help them understand different perspectives on common problems and issues and understand the wider context

- the opportunity to produce products and outputs that are better than those they could create by working alone
- collaboration with others to explore authentic problems and develop skills relevant to the digital workplace.

In this case study the tutor, like many others, was initially anxious about group work in live online learning, but soon became an advocate for the approach.

> I was apprehensive at first about using breakout rooms. I wasn't sure if groups would engage with the activities I'd set or whether the time I had allowed would be enough for them to complete the tasks. Now I really like using breakout rooms. They give me a chance to catch my breath and take a break and they give learners a real sense of control and a chance to interact. Often their feedback at the end of a session is that the discussions they have had with peers in small groups have been the most useful and interesting part. That's fine with me – I see myself as a 'guide on the side' rather than a 'sage on the stage', so if their learning comes from each other, that's just great.

There are many technological options to support online collaboration, including discussion forums, wikis, blogs and social networking tools. Most of these permit asynchronous collaboration which extends conversations over time, but the real time nature of web conferencing replicates face to face communication and discussion more effectively. Web conferencing also offers the opportunity for integration of other tools for group activity, for example application sharing or web touring. These benefits allow distributed group members to explore resources, solve problems, and create products together.

Preparing for group work

To support collaboration in a virtual classroom a facilitator needs to be able to create and manage spaces for group work, ensure that learners are confident with the technology, and design activities that encourage interaction and discussion. Facilitation during activities can sometimes be minimal, as effective groups will often work autonomously, but preparation and planning is key to success. Table 7.1 summarises some of the questions that need to be considered during planning.

Table 7.1 Questions for consideration during planning

Issue	Question
Creating and managing spaces for group work	What options for setting up breakout rooms does my software provide? Can breakout rooms be renamed to suit an activity or participants? If learners need access to their own virtual classroom for group work how can these be set up and what tools will learners have access to?
Design of activities	Will breakout rooms need to be ready in advance or set up during an activity? How will groups of participants be created? How will breakout rooms be used during the activity?
Providing learner support	Can participants move themselves in and out of breakout rooms, and do they know how to do this? How will participants know what to do when they reach a breakout room so they can get started on a task? How will learners get help and support during activities? Will learners know what to do at the end of a group task?

Creating and managing breakout rooms

The technical challenges associated with using breakout rooms are generally minimal. Once the way in which breakout rooms are created has been identified, it takes only a few seconds to get started in most web conferencing packages. Whilst many facilitators will set up breakout rooms in advance, it is usually possible to set them up whilst a session is in progress. This provides enormous flexibility in situations:

- where a group activity might be immediately required
- when participant numbers are not as expected
- where learners request opportunities for discussion
- where several different configurations of groups are used during a single session.

By default most software will label your breakout rooms Room 1, Room 2, Room 3, or A, B, C. You will probably have control over how many rooms you create and if it is possible to edit the names, more interesting titles can be allocated. Exciting room names may help generate a sense of anticipation or curiosity amongst learners. What will take place in the 'green room' or the 'Mackintosh room'? Descriptive names may help learners understand where they need to go or what a particular space is for. A room labelled 'the tutor's office' might be set up this way for private discussions. Alternatively if a group has a name, providing a breakout room with the same name gives a sense of ownership and purpose. Rooms could also be named to reflect different roles in a role play, different sides in a debate activity, or different theoretical ideas that will be discussed in each one.

Some thought needs to be given in advance to how you intend learners to move into rooms. Whilst most software packages offer functions which allow random allocation of participants to rooms or equal distribution of participants, these may not be appropriate in a learning context. Some of these tools may have been created with virtual meetings or large scale commercial webinars in mind. For learners the experience of being automatically uprooted from a busy main room and then unexpectedly finding themselves in a silent breakout room can be worrying and disorienting, particularly if they are unclear about what they should do once they get there. One option is for the facilitator to be in charge of moving participants around for each group activity. This can be time consuming and may generate a reliance on the facilitator since it takes away learners' autonomy and responsibility for their actions. Feedback from our own learners has suggested that they feel most comfortable when they have a sense of control over what is going on in a virtual classroom (Cornelius and Gordon, 2012). Ensuring that participants have the skills required to move themselves around between breakout rooms and get started on a task is, therefore, important. It may be appropriate to amend software settings to provide them with permission to use the tools they will need and give them a sense of control.

If learners are required to work in completely separate virtual classrooms, for example at times in between tutor led sessions, then these need to be set up and made available. Issues such as how learners will find these spaces, what tools they will have available, and who will moderate, need to be thought through and discussed with learners. Even if you set up alternative virtual classrooms it may be the case that learners have their own preferences for online collaboration. Undergraduates have been observed using Facebook to organise classroom-related collaborative activity (Lampe et al., 2011) and it follows that online learners will probably also use Facebook rather than their institutional virtual learning environment for group work, or prefer Skype or Google Hangouts to the institutionally provided virtual classroom for out of class collaboration. Whilst these choices should be respected, it is important to ensure that group decisions do not create problems for individual learners, and it may be appropriate to advocate the use of the institutionally provided tools as these guarantee equal access and a supported environment.

Creating the groups

In a face to face situation the allocation of students to groups may be dictated by logistical or practical considerations. In a lecture theatre it is difficult to work with any learners other than those next to you or immediately in front or behind. Groups of two or four therefore work well and can be created with minimal disturbance. In a workshop-style room it is possible to move furniture around and for participants to also move around freely. Groups can be set up and reconfigured more flexibly and quickly, although moving between groups can be disruptive and time consuming. A virtual classroom offers much more flexibility and efficiency. Groups of two are possible, and so are groups of ten or twenty, all within the same session. In practice, groups of three or four students work well if all are required to contribute. This allows everyone to keep their microphone or video switched on and facilitates communication in a style similar to a normal conversation. Moving around between groups requires just a few clicks of the mouse, and there is no opportunity for learners to get distracted or chat with their peers along the way.

If you use group work in face to face settings you probably already use a range of strategies to distribute learners into groups. Some of these might transfer to a virtual classroom setting, some may need adaptation, and some new strategies might be helpful. Table 7.2 suggests some group-formation strategies that we have successfully used during live online sessions.

As in any setting you may wish to influence the group creation process, for example to ensure that friends do not work together too often, or that a range of skills are present within each group. This 'tutor's choice' approach is another potential strategy and allows some additional issues specific to a virtual classroom to be considered. For example, you may wish to ensure that there is someone with competence and confidence with the technology in each group. If there are participants who can only interact using text due to audio problems, it may be best to put these people together so that the whole group relies on text chat. Alternatively, you may wish to distribute these participants amongst other groups to encourage the use of different media. With international groups, communication in a common language may also be a challenge, and may need to be taken into account to ensure that all participants can contribute to group discussions, and that appropriate support can be made available. The location of participants may be important if sustained independent group work is to be undertaken, since groups which are distributed across time zones may find it difficult to schedule convenient meeting times.

Table 7.2 Group creation strategies

Strategy	Description
Create groups based on the participant list	The first three participants in the list form Group 1, the second three form Group 2, and so on. Alternatively, participants can be allocated numbers based on their place in the list and allocated to odd number or even number groups. These are quick and easy approaches that can be adapted to any size of group. They are easy to facilitate and do not require any interaction from participants. However, you may need to watch the participant list, since actions in some virtual classrooms (such as raising a hand to ask a question) can disrupt the order of the list. Working from a printed or on-screen document may be helpful. If this approach is overused it may become tiresome and lead to the same participants repeatedly working together.
A virtual 'line up'	In a face to face classroom participants can be asked to move around to stand in a line based on a particular characteristic. For example one side of the classroom might represent January 1 and the other December 31 and participants asked to line up based on their birth date. Distance travelled to a session could also be used. Creative use of the whiteboard and drawing tools allows online versions of these activities. For example clip art or other annotations can be placed along a line to create an order. Once the order is established, participants can be divided up into groups. If birth dates are used 'seasons' or 'months' could be used to form groups. This approach can be fun and promotes interaction between participants, but may also be time consuming and require some flexibility from you as facilitator. For instance, if there are no birthdays in June or July the 'summer' group may be too small to be practicable. The strategy used should be designed with sensitivity to participants' needs and characteristics.
Pick a card	This strategy requires two whiteboards. The first contains enough blank card shapes for each participant to select one and write their name on it using the drawing tools. Participants are asked to remember which card they have selected, then a second screen is displayed with the cards 'flipped over' to reveal their colour. All learners who picked red cards become one group, all learners who picked blue cards become another, and so on. This approach takes a little preparation and may require some flexibility if participant numbers are not as expected. However, it is quick and efficient, and provides an opportunity to engage all participants for a short time.
Pick a number	This is similar to the 'pick a card' approach, but easier to implement. A screen with numbers written on it is displayed and learners write their name next to one of their choice. Groups can then be created using odd and even numbers, numbers divisible by 3 or whatever strategy is appropriate to create the desired number of groups.
Topic-based groups	Participants write their names next to potential topic areas presented on the screen and a group is created for each one. A more anonymous alternative is to ask participants to write topics of interest on the whiteboard and then reorganise these to create groups. If very disparate size groups result, final group composition may need to be discussed and negotiated. These are useful approaches where groups are being created for longer term collaborative activities.

Examples of group activities

Four examples of group activities which make use of breakout rooms are presented below. These could be adapted to your own context. The first three examples provide a progressive set of group activities which might work well if used sequentially during a course of study. The first is relatively straightforward in terms of process and the use of the technology, and allows the tutor to retain a level of control over the process. By the third activity, learners have considerably more independence and take the lead in what is going on, collaborating within and beyond tutor led sessions. The final example is an innovative use of breakout rooms for an introductory activity, although this could be adapted for other times during a session. In each example, the emphasis is on peers learning from each other and the facilitator role is principally to set up the activity (both technically and through clear instructions) and then provide guidance and opportunities for feedback and formative assessment through discussion.

Example 1: Discussion activity

This is probably one of the most common uses of breakout rooms. Small groups are created and then each allocated their own room in which to discuss a question, solve a problem or discuss an image provided by the facilitator. After an appropriate period for collaborative working, the breakout groups then report back to the main group, perhaps using a whiteboard slide they have prepared during their group time. Finkelstein (2006) calls these 'stone soup' activities, based on a fable of the same name. Following a prompt or directions from the facilitator each participant brings 'something to the table' for the small-group discussion in a breakout room. It 'cooks' during this discussion before it is shared with the full class. Collaboration in this way can lead to co-creation of resources and provides learner led activity during a session. Following their discussion groups might suggest topics for an agenda, resources for further discussion, or activities they wish to pursue.

The facilitator may need to consider the following issues:

- The time allowed for breakout group discussions should allow for a little 'settling in' time. It might be necessary for the group to introduce themselves and agree on a way of working together (for example using microphones all switched on at once, taking turns to speak, or using the chat tool) and ensure there is a shared understanding of their task. Discussions in a virtual classroom invariably need a little more time than those in face to face contexts.

- Reminders sent as announcements to the whole group can be very helpful, for example to alert participants that there are only five minutes left before they need to share their outcome with the rest of the group, or to remind them what the expectations are.
- Composition of groups might be carefully planned if these activities are undertaken early in a course. For example, in the early stages it may be helpful to have someone who is confident with the technology in each group. This can lead to peer support and may provide less confident learners with an opportunity to ask for help in a safer, less public space than the main classroom. Later in a course allocation to groups can be more varied, although it may be necessary to consider particular learner needs and preferences.
- Creating groups where communication can only take place using text can be an interesting experience for learners. If they are used to talking freely, taking away this ability can result in a heightened appreciation of issues faced by other learners.
- The facilitator may need to know how to copy whiteboards to breakout rooms, and back into the main discussion room. Preparation of breakout rooms can be done in advance so that instructions are available on whiteboard slides, but copying any notes made by each group back to the plenary room will need to be done during a session. An alternative, but potentially more time consuming, approach would be to tour around each group's breakout room and discuss their products in situ.

In the following case study the facilitator reflects on some of the strategies that make discussion activities effective.

I use a lot of discussion activities which involve learners spending time in small groups in breakout rooms. On some courses I try to bring them in right from the start and include them in the first online session. I think this helps to set the expectation that participants will have to interact with each other and take some responsibility in the virtual classroom rather than just sit back and listen to me. It is also good to give them space early in the course to air anxieties with each other as they would during informal conversations in a face to face setting. If they can do this in small groups in breakout rooms it means that they don't have to reveal insecurities to the whole group and they also start to identify with their peers who have similar issues. There has to be a clear purpose to any discussion activity and it is helpful to specify the product that groups should be working towards. This might be three key points on a whiteboard, a summary of their discussion or something more substantive such as a poster. Allocating roles, or better still, getting students to decide who will do what, is also helpful. Often there needs to be a scribe who will record the discussion on the whiteboard, someone to keep track of time and someone to report back at the plenary stage. If students are clear about what they need to do this helps groups get started quickly and leads to better outcomes.

Example 2: Jigsaw activity

A jigsaw activity involves creating a number of small groups who each undertake a distinct activity, then reconfiguring the groups to allow reporting and discussion with different peers. For example, three groups of three participants could be asked to review web sites on learning theories (see Figure 7.1). Each group has a different theory to examine and group discussion helps each individual prepare to talk about their theory to peers in other

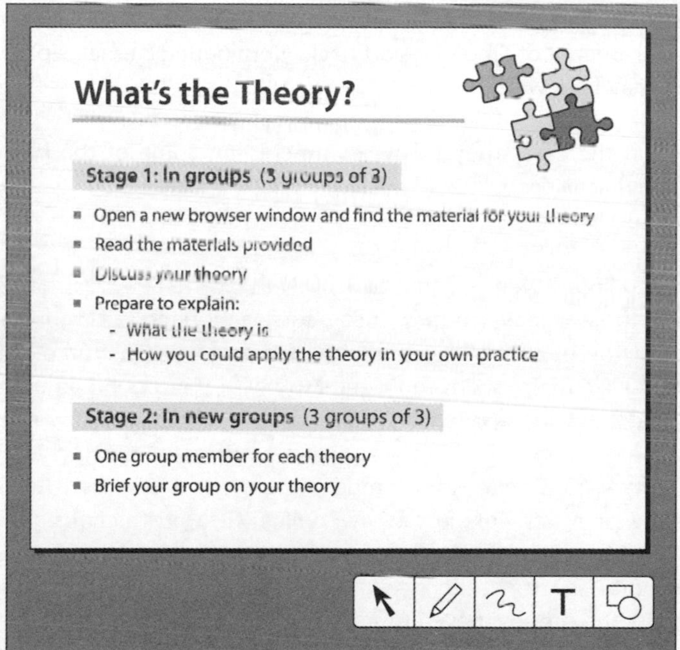

Figure 7.1 Instructions for jigsaw activity addressing educational theories for nine participants

groups. After an appropriate time, the groups reconvene so that three new groups of three are created, with each theory represented in each. Learners take turns to talk about the theory they have researched, and others are free to ask questions and widen the discussion. This activity takes the focus away from the facilitator as participants research, present and discuss content. Compared to a more traditional lecture approach that might involve a presenter talking through PowerPoint slides for each of the learning theories, this approach engages all participants and makes each one an important piece of the puzzle; they must complete their task in order to create the full picture for everyone.

The facilitator may need to consider the following issues:

- Preparation involves setting up appropriate breakout rooms, and possibly identifying resources that learners can access during a session.
- Group numbers can be difficult to work out, particularly if learners are unexpectedly absent or attendance is difficult to predict. It is best to plan the activity for, for instance, 12 (four groups of three) or 10 (five groups of two). A group of 11 will create problems and roles will have to be duplicated.
- Timing is important. In the second stage each learner should be allocated an equal amount of time to report back. Nominating a timekeeper in each group may help with this.

The tutor in the case study below comments on some of the benefits of online jigsaw activities.

> I have used jigsaw type activities effectively in face to face classrooms and really like the way in which they encourage everyone to see themselves as a piece of the puzzle. Each learner is important and has to contribute. Those who like to 'freeload' can't get away with that during jigsaw activities – they have to participate. Because they need to present what they have done to the new group they have to participate in the first stage of the activity – it's a great way of motivating them. I'm pleased to report that jigsaw activities work just as well online! Clear instructions are really important though, otherwise people get confused during the changeover between groups. In a face to face setting this results in chatter and disruption whilst the groups move around the room to reform, but if you can get it right with breakout rooms, the move to a new group is quick and efficient. Another advantage of online jigsaws is that learners can bring in their own resources. In a face to face setting I normally provide copies of

articles as resources for groups, but online I provide a few appropriate 'starter' web links. Learners can supplement these by doing some searches of their own and it is sometimes amazing to see what they can find in a short space of time.

Example 3: The poster activity

This is a complex activity that requires a degree of learner confidence and autonomy. Before the poster session, small groups collaborate to produce a digital 'poster' that they can display in the virtual classroom. The facilitator creates breakout rooms in advance – one for each group – and uploads the posters, or asks group members to do so.

During the session a two stage 'tour' is undertaken.

- **Stage 1: quick tour** – each group visits the posters created by other groups and spends a few minutes discussing them and generating questions to ask the authors. Groups move around the rooms in turn until all posters have been viewed.
- **Stage 2: slow tour** – all participants move to the first group's room. The group are given a few minutes to talk about their poster and then they receive questions from peers and a more general discussion follows. All participants then move to the second group's poster and the presentation/questions/discussion is repeated.

Figure 7.2 provides an example of an instruction slide for a poster activity.

The facilitator's role is to help set up groups and explain the requirements of the task. Otherwise this is a highly learner led activity in which participants can be allowed to select their own topics, undertake research independently and create a group product which they share and discuss with their peers The content of the session can come entirely from the participants.

When designing poster activities the facilitator needs to consider the following issues.

- A high degree of responsibility is placed on learners. They can be allowed to moderate the discussion about their posters rather than the facilitator fulfilling this role. However, if they do not prepare their posters in advance, the activity is compromised.
- The tutor's role is mainly to set the context, support interactions, keep learners focused and summarise or make connections with other course content. Especially satisfying is the situation where learners moderate

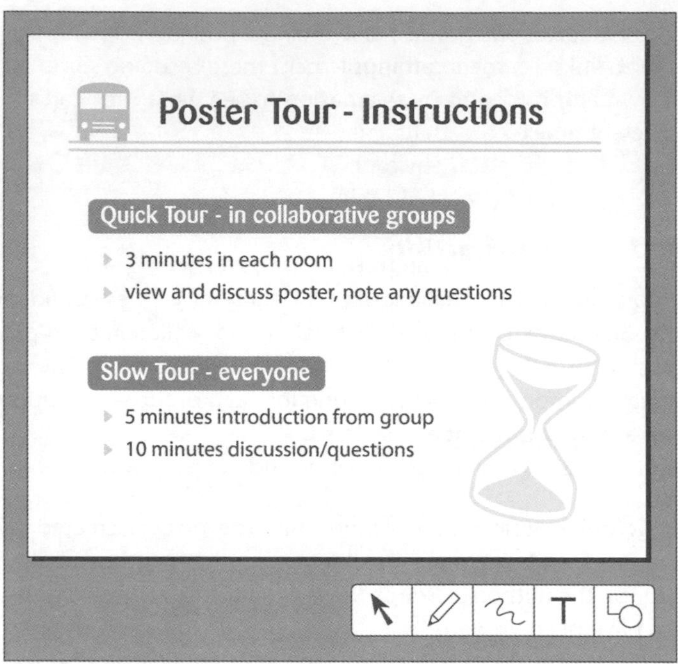

Figure 7.2 Poster tour instructions

their own discussions and whole-group dialogue takes place learner to learner rather than always through the tutor.

The tutor in the following case study reflects on her experience of facilitating this activity.

> It worked really, really well because of the way in which the groups engaged with each other and because of the way they had prepared for the activity. What they presented was very well structured, well thought through and in the best of the groups they had decided who was going to talk about which aspects of their poster presentation. The group that did particularly well used the online room in their own time to try out what they were going to present. I also think the engagement was very good. First of all learners were choosing something that was of interest to them. They were willing to work with one another beyond the timescale of synchronous tutorials. But it was the engagement of others as well who were interested to hear what they were presenting and willing to question them. I think part of the success was probably to do with ownership of

that activity in that it really was handed over to the learners. Keeping the timing right and not allowing things to drift was important. The timer can be very useful for that, and by that stage of the course participants were well used to attending to that. They kept their own timings correct as well. I guess in a classroom environment they could put posters up. They could still do the discussions but I think with web conferencing you've got questions also going on in the chat box. These allowed their presentation to continue without it being interrupted by questioning but they could go back and attend to the questions afterwards.

Example 4: 'Speed dating'

This is an activity which uses the idea of 'speed dating' or 'speed networking' in which you get just a few minutes to make a 'pitch' to another individual. It can be adapted to many different situations, but here we explain how it is used for an introductory activity to encourage interaction and help learners get to know each other.

Numbered breakout rooms are set up so that there are enough for students to work together in pairs. A prompt for discussion is provided, for example 'What would you like to get out of the course?' or 'What is the question you want to answer in your own research?' One person is given two or three minutes to talk with the other listening and asking questions. At the end of the allocated time the roles swap over and the new speaker talks for two or three minutes. At the end of this 'round' one of the participants moves to another room so that new pairs are formed. Once again the pair take it in turns to speak and listen.

The activity continues until all pairs have met, or, in a larger group, until three or four rounds have been completed. Although this might seem repetitive, the opportunity to repeatedly articulate ideas can be beneficial for learners and help them shape up emerging thoughts or develop verbal communication skills.

When using 'speed dating' the following issues may need to be considered.

- The facilitator needs to provide precise instructions to prevent confusion over moving rooms. It can be confusing for someone to be left in a room on their own and it may disrupt the activity if too many people arrive in one space. Perhaps give an extra minute for changeovers during the first round or have a practice round to ensure that everyone knows what they are doing.

- This activity can work better online than an equivalent face to face activity. Moving rooms is easy and efficient, and there are no distractions or opportunities to 'chat' during the changeover periods.
- It may be necessary to use the chat tool and audio to involve everyone. If chat is needed by some participants, it may be helpful to increase the time allowed since most people type more slowly than they speak.
- Efficient and consistent timings are important and participants need to know what they should do when the timer sounds. The announcement facility might be helpful to capture everyone's attention.

Here are three tutors' reflections on facilitating a 'speed dating' activity – with varying levels of success.

> The sheer organisation of the 'speed dating' activity, where one person stays put and others move around, trying to get that across to people, I found difficult. I lost the thread, too, of where I was meant to be. I ended up just cracking up laughing, because it got so chaotic and out of hand!

> We got some interesting feedback from some of the students, including someone who ended up in a room on their own, with no-one to speak to. That's the sort of thing that's quite challenging for a new facilitator, and perhaps a challenge too far for someone at an early stage.

> I had a really positive experience with the 'speed dating' activity. I used it with a small group of eight postgraduate students working on their dissertation projects, and asked them all to talk for a few minutes about their research ideas. I set up the four breakout rooms with individual names: 'Ian's room', 'Claire's room' and so on, and we had a little joke about this probably being the first time they had had a room named after them! Participants really seemed to appreciate the opportunity to articulate their early project ideas in this private setting and commented that it helped them clarify and develop their ideas.

▶ Facilitating group activities

The four activities above provide a glimpse into the wide range of ways that breakout rooms can be used to allow learners to collaborate, and some of the issues that might arise for facilitators. With creativity and a bit of confidence you should be able to design other activities for your own learners. To help ensure success:

- start simple, building up learners' confidence gradually
- consider learners' needs and preferences
- provide clear instructions
- allocate more time than you think you need
- monitor interactions and participation.

Learners may need support to help them to build their confidence with online group work. They may be unaccustomed to activities involving discussion and collaboration, so the best strategy is to start small and simple before building up to more complex, learner led activities. It might be appropriate to start with a short breakout group discussion following which the group provide verbal input to a plenary session. A volunteer could be invited to feed back on behalf of the group if there are some confident learners in the group. At the next session a group discussion could be used to generate a whiteboard slide summarising points raised or the solution to a problem. Gradually, a wider range of learners can be invited to contribute to whole group feedback. As confidence in the virtual classroom grows, more complex activities could be introduced, such as those involving changes of room or learner led discussions.

As part of the support provided learners should know how to ask for help when they are in breakout rooms. Let them know if you want them to wait for you to drop in, whether they should send you a message using the chat tool, or if they should use the hand raising tool to attract your attention. This tutor below found that she needed to remind her participants how to ask for help, and also develop her own skills with the tools to support group work.

> It's useful to alert students to the fact that if they put their hand up in the breakout room you will see their raised hand and will go to them, but remember to say that before they go to the breakout room. The other thing I've learned to use is the announcements, but the number of times I've wasted an announcement because I've forgotten to tick the little box

> that says 'send to all rooms'. It's just so frustrating, I do it and I think 'I've done it again'.

Learners' needs and preferences for mode of communication should always be considered during group work. If a learner uses text as an alternative to audio it may be necessary to remind other group members to monitor the chat tool. Some groups will be entirely comfortable working with multiple media whilst others may prefer to restrict the media being used whilst they get used to leading their own learning.

As some group activities can be complex, the way in which instructions are provided is important. Most facilitators give verbal instructions and supplement these with information displayed on the whiteboard. Copying the whiteboards into breakout rooms so that learners do not lose sight of instructions when they move to their rooms is helpful. The clarity and order of instructions is critical. Saying 'I want you to move to your breakout rooms …', before you have given details of the task may create chaos since some participants will move before you have finished speaking. If they miss the instructions you will need to 'chase' them around the virtual classroom to ensure that they know what they are required to do. It is important to be much clearer about the sequence of actions and sequence of instructions than you would be in a face to face situation. You should also provide time for participants to ask questions before they are sent off to their groups. Effective group work requires careful planning and preparation along with clear instructions.

The need to keep track of time in a virtual classroom has been mentioned in previous chapters, since it is easy for live online activities to take longer than expected. You might be interrupted by technical issues, or delayed when instructions have to be repeated. The timer tool is very useful to help manage the time taken for setting up group work, for the group collaboration itself, and for any follow up plenary discussions. Keeping plenary feedback sessions to time can be particularly challenging when groups have a lot to share and everyone wants to contribute. Using strategies that ensure that all groups are given their chance to report back and receive feedback from the tutor and peers is important. Timings should be carefully allocated to permit this. Timing may be particularly important if any component of the discussion is being assessed. In this case it may be wise not to plan the plenary discussion at the very end of a session, but include instead a less important activity that can be abandoned if discussions take longer than expected.

This tutor expresses her concerns over time allocations for group work and highlights the importance of sharing expectations about time with students.

My most recent class spent a lot of time rehearsing their timings before giving a presentation. One group had a lot of slides which they sent to me to have a look. I sent back a message to say 'are you sure this is going to work in the time you've got?' but they said 'oh yes we've rehearsed it, so many seconds for this one and for that one'. They had really done very careful preparation to use their time. They were so aware that in the session the timing had become absolutely critical to the way they moved through the pace of the activities, so I think something about that transfers the real power into the participants as they deliver their presentation. They know that for twenty minutes they have the floor.

Sending groups off into breakout rooms can be a little unnerving for a facilitator since it decreases the already limited feedback available. Monitoring group activities is made easier when software tools provide clues about interactions, as the example in Figure 7.3 shows.

Even with these tools available it can still be a challenge for a single facilitator to know what is going on in a number of breakout rooms. Some of the learners who participated in our research were asked how they felt about the tutor visiting breakout rooms. One learner noticed, but did not feel it necessary to acknowledge the tutor's presence, another said she did not notice unless someone said something. Overall the impression given was that learners did not mind tutor visits and actually found it helpful to have the tutor drop in to answer questions. A breakout room provides a more private opportunity for this than when the whole group are present in the main room (Cornelius and Gordon, 2012).

Depending on the nature of your own learners, the way in which you monitor group activity might be something to negotiate or discuss with participants to ensure that everyone is aware of and comfortable with your actions. This tutor explains her strategies for monitoring interaction.

Figure 7.3 The participant window showing tools used by learners in breakout rooms

It's always reassuring to see the microphone symbols come on in each of the rooms so that I know people are communicating, but it's difficult to know what they are talking about. When you are in a face to face classroom you can listen in to discussions unobtrusively, and intervene if you hear misunderstandings or if things are going too far off-topic. But I know from face to face experience that if I 'tour' groups soon after getting them started they will come to expect this and sometimes chat socially whilst waiting for me to come along to remind them of the instructions and nudge them to get going. I don't mind a bit of social chat, and it's great to hear a bit of laughter from time to time. Usually when I drop in the focus is on the topic or activity.

This tutor talks about being able to see whether microphones are switched on or off within a breakout room. It is often also possible to see if other tools, for example whiteboard drawing tools or application sharing, are being used within a breakout room so that you can get an impression of what is taking place without needing to visit. Steed (2011) suggests that breakout rooms provide an opportunity for learners to learn by discovering things for themselves and this can be facilitated if monitoring is done remotely rather than through frequent visits.

Some group activities require learners to collaborate between tutor led sessions. For this collaboration groups may need private virtual classrooms to work in, between formal sessions. If this is the case, it may be beneficial to ensure that a more confident virtual classroom user is included in each group to help support others. The outcomes of learner led collaboration can be impressive, and learners may reveal and share skills and resolve problems without the tutor present. In the case of the poster activity discussed above, groups have been observed developing their skills and autonomy in their own virtual classrooms, but also their skills with other software packages through the use of file sharing.

Monitoring student participation during group activities is a perennial challenge. In a face to face group it may become obvious if someone is not contributing to group discussion, or not fulfilling their obligations to the group. This can be much more difficult to spot online. For example, when observing a group discussion from outside their room, microphone use symbols may make it look as if someone is speaking, but they may have (intentionally or unintentionally) left their microphone switched on. Group work in learner led sessions is difficult to monitor, and it is easy for a reluctant participant to claim technical problems or mistakes over time as an excuse for not joining in. Sometimes the reluctant participant will make things more stressful for peers by then ignoring or failing to respond to email inquiries or their requests to join sessions. In any group situation those who do not pull their weight are frustrating, but for a group working solely online, it can be extremely difficult to deal with a 'no show' or minimalist contributor. It is important for the facilitator to be alert to the possibility of minimalist contributions and monitor group work, perhaps by asking for regular progress reports, or making informal enquiries about progress at online sessions. Careful design of activities, so that there is a link to assessment or clear benefit and outcome from contribution may also help. The successful poster activity described above was not formally assessed, but the research and discussions undertaken as part of the collaborative endeavours to create this were required in a subsequent individually assessed task. This approach was used to encourage contributions from all group members.

Finally, participants need to know when to emerge from their breakout rooms. A clear explanation of how they will know when their time in the room has ended is helpful. The timer tool is useful for this, and it may also be possible to send reminder 'announcements'. Learners need to know what they are expected to do at the end of the task. Do they wait for the facilitator to visit their breakout room and tell them? Do they return automatically to the main room for the next instruction? Or are they expected to move on to another room for the next part of a task? Without a clear explanation of the actions you wish them to take before the activity starts, confusion may result, and participants may not know where to go. When things start to go awry there can be a huge temptation to resort to selecting the option which automatically moves everyone back to the main room. However, using this will reduce learners' sense of control and responsibility in the environment.

Learner led group work

As part of an online course learners may need to work together as a group outside scheduled class sessions. Giving them access to a virtual classroom of their own provides an option for them to collaborate, providing it can be set up to allow them to do what they need to do. In some web conferencing systems, only facilitators can perform certain functions, such as uploading or sharing files, or creating breakout rooms. If it is not possible for learners to be given appropriate status to undertake these tasks themselves, then they may be unable to collaborate effectively in their own spaces. However, if appropriate permissions can be set up there are a number of tools which are particularly helpful for collaborative tasks. These include web tours, file

Table 7.3 Virtual classroom tools that support collaborative activities

Tool	Description
Web tours	Web conferencing systems usually allow everyone in a room to 'follow' an individual, usually the facilitator, as they explore the Internet. Everyone in a virtual classroom will see the same web pages and this creates an opportunity for discussion of online sites and sharing of knowledge about resources. Visits to some sites which have high technological requirements (such as YouTube) may be difficult to do in a live event since the bandwidth available to individuals will vary and there can be organisational firewall issues to overcome. However, these restrictions can often be overcome by using alternative tools for collaboration.
File exchange	Tools may be available which allow files to be uploaded to the virtual classroom so that participants can download a copy for themselves. Files in most formats can be exchanged this way for viewing or editing outside the virtual classroom. Learners might use this feature to exchange key documents or common reading materials.
Application and screen sharing	It may be possible to share an application, for example a word processor or spreadsheet, to allow collaborative creation and editing of resources. Some software also allows one user to share their entire screen with others in a session. Control over the application or screen is sometimes restricted to one user, although it may be possible to pass control to others.

exchange and application or screen sharing (Table 7.3). Although the tools available through web conferencing may not yet be as comprehensive or sophisticated as in those that are specifically designed for collaborative online working, they still provide useful options for co-creation.

Where learners have the ability to collaborate online there can be unanticipated benefits and outcomes, as this tutor describes in relation to the poster activity described earlier in this chapter.

> One group produced an amazing animated poster, way beyond the static PowerPoint style slide I was expecting. I asked them how they had managed to achieve this and it was clear that the opportunity to work together online in their own virtual classroom had been really important. One group member had been able to show others some software he had on his own computer that he thought they could use for creating a poster. He used application sharing to do this. I think he also showed some examples of animated posters by taking them all on a web tour. Once the group had agreed to try out the animated poster approach they documented their design ideas on a shared PowerPoint slide. The group

member with access to the specialist software produced a first draft of the poster and used application sharing again to test it out and get comments and feedback from his peers. It was obvious that the activity had a significant impact on the IT skills of some of the group members, and they were all much more confident with the web conferencing tools in later class sessions.

IN SUMMARY

Group work is a strategy which supports interaction and dialogue, provides variety in online sessions, develops learners' confidence, and promotes autonomy in the virtual classroom. It allows collaboration and through this engages learners in the co-creation of resources that shape their own learning. Facilitating group work may seem challenging at first, raising anxieties about what is going on when learners move into their own online spaces, but with time and practice it becomes possible to provide an effective learner led experience using strategies which encourage collaboration. This chapter has provided examples of activities which have been successfully implemented in a virtual classroom and has raised some of the issues which need to be considered when planning group work. These include:

- **Making appropriate technical preparations** – you need to be familiar with breakout room tools and the ways in which the actions of participants in breakout rooms can be monitored remotely. The ability to copy and move resources, such as whiteboard screens, between breakout rooms may be useful. Tools for posting text chat messages to different rooms are also very helpful. Confidence is also needed with tools that allow collaborative working, such as file and application sharing.
- **Creating appropriate groups** – the creation of a group that can work together effectively with the media available is important. Consideration of the needs of learners and the opportunities they have available should inform decisions about group composition. A variety of strategies can be used to create groups that also encourage interaction and dialogue between learners.
- **Designing meaningful activities** – many approaches that work in face to face settings can be adapted for the virtual classroom, as the examples provided demonstrate. Clear instructions are always

important online, particularly where group activities go beyond the simple discussion group format. Issues such as the roles students will take in groups, timing of tasks, and feedback strategies should also be considered during design.

- **Facilitating effectively** – although the facilitation of group work can be very 'hands off' once an activity is under way, you have an important role to play in terms of monitoring participation and interaction. Providing clear instructions, being available to provide help and support, and keeping an eye out for those who contribute minimally are all important tasks during group activities.
- **Encouraging autonomy** – distributed groups of learners can be given access to a range of tools that support learner led activity using web conferencing. They need to be prepared for this, and generally value the opportunity to interact with peers using break-out rooms or in their own virtual classroom without a tutor or trainer present.

In any context, and with any new group of learners the facilitator should start with simple group activities and work towards more complex tasks, building learners' confidence and skills along the way.

8 Assessment for learning

Assessment may be regarded as the end of learning, the final test to confirm competence or knowledge. A broader definition of assessment encompasses it as part of the learning process, helping learner motivation, confirming understanding and offering stepping stones to different levels of understanding. Online learning is particularly dependent on this broad view of assessment. The purpose of this chapter is to explore:

- student centred learning and assessment
- assessment as a marker of progress
- assessment and learner confidence
- assessment and exploration
- web conferencing for learning and assessment
- assessment in the virtual classroom
- assessment outside the virtual classroom
- the assessor: student, peer and tutor
- the online learner as assessor
- friends and colleagues as assessors
- the online facilitator as assessor.

Student centred learning and assessment

The learner centred approach requires a match between the assessments which are included in a live online learning session and learner needs (Brown and Race, 2012). There are some common student needs which link with assessment.

- Most learners have a goal and therefore benefit from assessment which helps them to achieve their goal by marking progress along the way and confirming achievement at the end.
- Most learners need to gain confidence in a new subject area and therefore benefit from assessment which is achievable and gives them a sense of progress.
- Most learners need to interrogate new subject matter to test out their understanding. Assessment is most valuable if it offers this exploratory experience.

Assessment as a marker of progress

The virtual classroom is a more comfortable place for learners if there are signposts and markers of progress to guide them. These include strategies for giving learners a sense that this is their place and they have a right to be there. We have already mentioned the use of a welcome message and a familiar way of starting the online session to help them to feel more at ease. The use of familiar ways of testing learning can also help learners to feel at ease with assessment. Additionally, if the structure of the course reflects assessment requirements, learners have a sense of progression and are likely to feel more confident about the process of being assessed.

When the schedule of dates is issued at the beginning of a new course, it usually includes the dates for assessment. This provides a structure for the course, by dividing learning in a way that ensures learners achieve their goal and have all the skills and knowledge that they need by the time of the deadline. This structure is particularly important for online learners. They have often chosen to study online because they have limited time for study and a definite motivation to be successful. It can be very helpful if the schedule for assessment appears on screen regularly and reminders are provided about the way that learning will be structured in order to be ready for the assessment or deadline. The following example appeared in the corner of the whiteboard at each weekly workshop and was updated as each deadline passed.

Assessment schedule

Assignment 1 – to be completed by end of week 4

Assignment 2 – to be completed by end of week 8

Collaborative project – to be presented as a group at session 5

In order to avoid this type of visual signpost becoming too familiar so that participants cease to 'see' what is on screen, the tutor or trainer also has to offer signposts that show the structure of the course and the connection between that structure and the assessment. Here is an example of one tutor's reminder for students.

Just a reminder that this course is divided into three parts and there's an assignment at the end of each part. We'll begin by going over what we did in Part One and then I'll introduce the new material to be covered in Part Two. Just have a look at the schedule that I've put on the screen and check that you know the dates for completing assignments. This is quite a busy schedule, as it includes dates for asynchronous discussion forums as well as workshops. Hopefully, you can see that you've got about two weeks between each online session. There is self study material to complete in that time, which will prepare you for the assignment.

It can also be helpful if the facilitator asks the participants to interact with the information in some way, perhaps confirming one of the dates or checking a holiday. In any situation, it is possible for us to think we have got the message simply by reading something, only to discover later that we have forgotten important information. In the virtual classroom this can be particularly problematic, as participants lack the nonverbal clues and aids to memory that they would have in a face to face situation. It is also more difficult for the tutor to check understanding without these clues and to assume that everyone has grasped the information, when in fact that is not the case.

Participants can also measure their progress if the course includes familiar formative assessments on a regular basis in workshops and tutorials. The most common version of this is to test knowledge or skills that were acquired in the previous session. It is possible for the facilitator to simply recite the key points from that session and list them on screen. The disadvantage of this online is that there is no interaction with participants and no way of knowing if they have remembered what was covered in the previous session. It is much more helpful to include some kind of quiz or activity which tests participants' memory. It is also helpful to repeat the use of some visual aids from a previous session to offer a visual reminder.

Presentations and activities delivered in online workshops can integrate assessment in order to engage the learners in the learning process and offer participants ways of testing their memory and understanding. This increases their awareness that they are making progress or need to review their approach to learning. In a physical classroom, a familiar approach is to ask simple questions about key points, but online this may result in silence as individuals are reluctant to speak out spontaneously. Asking participants to put answers in the chat box or type them on screen gives the advantage of everyone being asked to do something and also offering a range of answers which can be compared and discussed. Simply asking participants to provide a few words in the chat box giving an opinion, or marks out of ten for their view of something, promotes interaction and lightly assesses engagement with the topic.

Assessment and learner confidence

The meaning that is attributed to assessment by both teachers and learners has a significant impact on the way assessment is experienced. After a stressful experience of assessment, it is easy to vow 'never again'. The implicit question in this kind of comment is 'why would I put myself through that again?' Assessment may not be stressful. It may not be difficult. The real barrier is often the way that learners perceive assessment and the baggage that is associated with the term itself.

In the online environment, fear of being assessed and judged has a powerful influence on the learner's ability to learn, and potentially on success in summative assessments. Without some kind of review of learners' understanding of course content or themes, it may be difficult for them to progress. In some of the massive online courses, thousands of learners follow the course and interaction with the tutor is very limited, but they still include quizzes and questions to help the learner to judge progress and go back over things that have not been well understood. Web conferencing has greater potential for interaction but perhaps the facilitator has to contend with the anxiety that being questioned or tested may provoke in participants. Making a success of assessing learning online is about helping learners to feel safe when learning is being tested, and to give them a sense of achievement and reward when they try to take part in any assessment process.

Learner confidence is often helped by praise or 'rewards' for successful participation and correct answers. Web conferencing systems usually have rewards built into their programs, such as a smiley face, a round of applause, or a gold star. Figure 8.1 shows some examples of praise icons.

These visual rewards probably offer a low level feel good factor. Many learning applications which can be used on mobile devices include similar rewards when the user wins a point or is successful in a test. For example, an application to teach piano tests the ability to read music and play the correct notes on the keyboard. The user tests himself against the clock, against his previous score and using more complex musical notation. He is given a score, a winner's cup, a rosette and a round of applause when each test ends. Initially, this can be amusing and motivating, but it can also become irritating and demotivating over time. Feedback which is most meaningful to an individual is usually focused and believable. Praise icons in

Figure 8.1 Examples of praise icons

web conferencing systems are believable and useful if they are used when praise is deserved rather than for every contribution. Encouraging other participants in a virtual classroom to offer praise has value too – it avoids too many speakers coming in at once, but allows participants to see that others are supporting them.

Assessment and exploration

Exploration may be a more useful word for some aspects of assessment. For example, a learning experience may start with a question which allows participants to explore their own experience to find connections with new learning. This allows them to construct new skills and understanding by making connections with what they already know. In the following example, the tutor wants participants to explore the impact of technology on social life in modern society.

> Let's take an imaginary journey from home to the shops. List all the technology that you meet along the way and that you use in the shop. Perhaps you start by locking your house and setting the digital burglar alarm. Maybe you get a text along the way asking you to get something else at the shops. Is there an electronic sign at the bus stop telling you how long you need to wait for a bus? Did you scan your own shopping or did the checkout assistant do it for you? Now you have a go and see how many items you can list.

This example focuses on what learners may already know. Is this assessment? For the learner it is probably better described as exploration, but for the tutor it is assessment of prior learning and experience, allowing the tutor to understand better what participants already know and what content will best meet their needs. This is particularly important if the online group is made up of people from different cultures or backgrounds, who may not share a common understanding. The example of the trip to the shops given above might be entirely unsuitable for learners from a rural area, or people living in remote places. The use of examples from the pretechnological age can also be problematic. In a similar situation to the one above, a tutor was trying to explain to a group of young students how people were paid before money could be transferred directly into a bank. The group had no sense that actual cash was handed over in envelopes, so the tutor 'assessed' their understanding and provided appropriate information to help them understand life before computers.

Exploration can also be about feelings and experiences that have changed an individual's perception. It is common to ask for participants in a workshop to give their reaction to a video clip, or a case study or some practical demonstration. This may lead to individuals telling stories from their own experience. The following example was from a participant in a session about stress management. The tutor made reference to cognitive behavioural therapy and asked the group if they had any knowledge of this. The following example was provided by one of her students.

> I lived in a village which experienced a terrible tragedy and everyone was offered counselling or some sort of therapy. I didn't feel I needed it, but agreed to go with a friend to a session described as cognitive behavioural therapy. It was much more helpful than I expected. The therapist described this technique where you imagine putting negative feelings in a box and putting them to one side, just for that day, and getting on with normal things. It's a technique that I've found helpful in other situations too.

This example is probably more memorable and meaningful for the group than an example provided by the tutor. It is also an assessment of individual participants' understanding of the topic, if the stories they tell reflect a connection with the topic. This process also allows for comparison of different experiences. Exploration of these differences is then assessed by the tutor in order to formulate a way of aligning different experiences with any theoretical perspectives or the course content.

Boundaries can also be explored in a group setting, perhaps by using case studies or problem solving activities which offer participants opportunities to comment on a range of unfamiliar experiences. An example of this is the professional–client relationship, where boundaries involving the relationship itself as well as issues such as confidentiality can be explored. The tutor or trainer is then able to assess the way in which individuals respond to the scenarios presented and the comments of other members of the group.

Exploratory approaches to teaching and learning online encompass assessment in a holistic way, so that learning and assessment are two sides of the same coin.

▶ Web conferencing for learning and assessment

Throughout this book, we have stressed that the technology is a tool which is only useful if the facilitator keeps learner needs in mind. This is particularly true when planning assessment for live online sessions. It is also likely that learners will have to use other types of technology for formal assessment of their work and this will have to be introduced during web conferencing sessions.

Assessment in the virtual classroom

We have already considered some aspects of assessment as part of the learning process which are well suited to the web conferencing environment. Assessment may also be necessary as part of course accreditation and to provide evidence of process as well as the final product. Live online learning provides a very good opportunity for gathering evidence about learners' performance because it is taking place in real time. The facilitator is able to authenticate contributions and observe a range of skills. Additionally, it is likely that the facilitator will know learners well and be able to support them during any assessment and perhaps reduce the fear factor a little. Here is an example from a tutor who was asked to authenticate distance learning students' work, without ever meeting the learners online.

> Every year the university would send me distance learning students' exam scripts and I had to sign a sheet saying that I believed it was the students' own work. I based my decision on their use of language and the type of work they had submitted for course assignments. It was a very difficult and worrying task – how could I be sure that this was their work when it was based on my memory of work that I had marked during the year?

In contrast, the following example describes the experience of a tutor who is able to assess participants in a virtual classroom.

> Each of the students gave a presentation to a small group in the breakout rooms. I went round the rooms and listened to the presentations, trying to catch something of each one. The participants in each group used a marking sheet for each presentation, based on criteria that they had drawn up themselves and I had agreed. It was far more successful than I expected. The students seemed more relaxed delivering presentations to their peers and the peer feedback was helpful to them, but I was able to listen in and be sure that everyone participated and was treated fairly by their peers.

Online assessment is being used more widely in all types of courses, including very practical subjects. An example of this is the use of online software to practise skills in dental training. It allows students to see the patient and practice carrying out virtual surgery, and also experience the impact on skin and bone as they move their instruments. Another example comes from an online course for stitched textiles. Stitching and creativity are assessed by using digital photographs to show each stage of the process and PowerPoint presentations to display finished items. Course tutors never actually see the items that their students have made. These innovative approaches to skills testing link well with the use of web conferencing. Assessment of skills can be carried out without travelling to an assessment centre. Here is a student nutritionist's account of this type of experience.

> My assessment task was to carry out an interview with a 'patient'. The rest of the students in my group observed me, but I also saw them taking a case. The 'patient' was an actor using a web cam. I could see her sitting in a chair and she was able to show me a skin rash on her arm. She could also see me and I had practiced using a web cam so that I was able to behave as normally as possible, particularly paying attention to my eye contact. I spent some time building a rapport with my 'patient' and then asked her some questions. It was a very comfortable experience for me despite the pressure of being assessed. The actor gave very positive feedback too.

These examples give some indication of the potential for carrying out a range of assessments using the virtual classroom as the assessment centre. A wide range of assessment approaches can be used, such as quizzes, filling in blanks and labelling items. It is also possible to be very creative and to make assessments relevant to online learners' experiences and background. Web conferencing also offers the facility to record many different types of assessment activity, and these recordings can be used for validation of assessment or revisiting assessment for quality assurance.

Assessment outside the virtual classroom

Web conferencing is just one of the new technologies which are revolutionising learning and assessment. It is likely that students who are taking a course online will also be expected to use online technology to submit assignments. We referred to the double learning experience for online students in an earlier chapter – not only do they have to learn a new subject, they also have to learn how to use the technology which supports their course. Here is an extract from a student journal which describes this experience.

> I can't take much more of this!!! First, we have to learn how to take part in activities in a virtual classroom. Then we have online discussion forums where we post messages to one another. Emails flood into my inbox from course organisers. My first assignment was to video myself and send it off to my tutor using web based sharing software – nightmare software more like! My first written assignment had to be submitted via plagiarism software. Results were sent through an online system that was like Fort Knox to access. I've got enough passwords to paper my living room – in fact that might be a good idea and then I'd have a quick way of finding them. So what's the final straw – we're going on a virtual field trip. What will I put in my suitcase ...

This example clearly shows that an important role for the online facilitator is to support learners to cope with all this technology. Telling students that it will be fine and that the technology is easy to use is not good enough! It is best if tutors and trainers are realistic about problems and offer helpful warnings in advance, so that learners know what to expect, and offer support if difficulties arise without making judgemental comments which leave the student feeling that they are in the wrong.

Allocating time during sessions in the virtual classroom for going over assignment requirements is only part of the task. Time also has to be given to describing and discussing how technology will be used in the assessment process. Screen shots of software which will be used help learners to visualise the process that they will go through when submitting assignments.

E-portfolios are commonly used by learners to collate materials for assessment, allowing them to store assessment items in an identifiable online folder. This can often be accessed directly by the tutor or the person marking the assignments, and feedback is given through the portfolio system. An additional benefit is that portfolios can be used to transfer assessment from one course to another or even to other institutions. Some professions now use e-portfolios to keep records of all professional development and career experiences, making the information available as part of professional accreditation or even to prospective employers. This use of e-portfolios may seem alarming to some users and tutors, but additional learning benefits have also been identified. Because past assignments are available to learners their knowledge and understanding can be progressive. Deeper insights may be gained into a topic by the use of reflective journals in an e-portfolio and thoughtful accumulation of evidence and ideas. A design tutor described this experience.

> Every time we complete a 3D design, the students place their work in their online portfolio. I visit each portfolio before we have a one to one session with students, but the real learning seems to come from their review of the items that they've stored, rather than mine. They can see progress over a period of time which is very encouraging and motivating for them. They also seem to be aware that the ability to see this development and analyse their own experience is also a valuable part of their learning. I don't think this was as clear to students when they kept paper portfolios.

The web conferencing facilitator may also have a significant role to play in the use of the other technologies which support a course. Whatever their subject specialism, almost all tutors and trainers now have to be able to teach the skills needed to use technology. Here are some reminders of ways to do this.

- If learners have to use any technology that is new to them, try it out first. Take screen shots of the different stages that you go through and check out what is required to gain access, such as passwords or additional software.
- If tutors have a different level of access, then ask for student access so that you can see what your students see.
- Provide students with written guidelines on how to access particular systems and check that these guidelines are accurate, then check again in the future in case there has been a system upgrade.
- Avoid making assumptions about technology – check that the technology does what everyone expects it to do.
- Avoid making assumptions about the learners, particularly the assumption that they will be able to use the technology intuitively.

Web conferencing and other learning technologies can be used to gather and store assessment evidence. A combination of careful management of the technology and supportive facilitation of the assessment process ensures that learners are able to make the best use of this assessment opportunity.

▶ The assessor: student, peer and tutor

The role of the tutor or trainer as the only assessor of learning is changing. Learners themselves, other participants in their course and colleagues at work or in other organisations may be involved in the assessment process. This can be very helpful in terms of reducing the feeling of being judged by an expert, and increasing the opportunity to share ideas and experiences.

The online learner as assessor

Completing a test and marking it as the answers are read out is a familiar approach and one of the earliest non-technological forms of self assessment. It includes the temptation to change answers in order to score better marks, but also heightens awareness of the right and wrong answers. Receiving a marked test back from a tutor often results in a quick look at the scores without considering how they were achieved. Self assessment is believed to be a most effective way of making learners active participants in the learning process (Boud, 1995). Research reports positive results for self assessment as a way of improving results in summative assessment, increasing reflection on learning and helping learners to take greater responsibility for their own learning (Dochy, Segers and Sluijsmans, 1999). Self assessment can be used online successfully to provide instant feedback on knowledge and a sense of progress – and to highlight the need for more study.

Self assessment can also be a creative process. If learners have produced a document or a poster or an artefact, they can assess their achievement against their own criteria or against criteria provided by the tutor. As a first line assessment it has the advantage of being private, open to amendment and closely linked to learners' sense of achievement, rather than someone else's view of what is successful or not. In a live online workshop, participants can go to a breakout room to create or display something that is theirs, and also evaluate their work. Web conferencing can provide each participant with their own room, in a way that is rarely possible using physical space. The tutor is able to visit the breakout rooms and hear what learners have to say about their work, without making any judgements or suggestions. When the group comes back together it is possible for them to share their own evaluations, without necessarily sharing their work. Alternatively, the work can be displayed in the main room and peers can offer comment after hearing the evaluation of the person who created the item.

Self assessment can also be part of a cumulative process. As each assessment is marked, feedback is added to previous feedback, providing a comprehensive account of all assignments completed. The earlier case study about 3D design students commented on the value of this form of self assessment. The process can begin with the learner providing initial comment and then, as others offer feedback, comparisons can be made with the learner's first impressions. The 'record' and 'save' facilities in web conferencing systems can be used to support this process, or the e-portfolio system mentioned earlier.

An element of competition in assessing learning can provide motivation, interest and fun, but it can also disadvantage the sensitive or reluctant learner who is unable to cope with comparison with others. Self assessment using web conferencing systems can be a way of improving the confidence of this type of learner and also increasing resilience when working with others. Here is some feedback from online learners on the experience of self assessment.

> I liked assessing my project in the breakout room. I displayed all my ideas on slides and then created a review page for my comments. The tutor called in and listened to me talking about what I was doing. He suggested an additional column in my review page, but otherwise seemed to trust me to carry out a systematic review of what I had created.

> I rarely spoke in our online workshops. I thought everyone else in the group was really clever and that I'd look stupid if I made a mistake. Assessing my own work changed that. It forced me to admit that I wasn't any different from others in the group – the evidence was there that I was able to do the calculations correctly just like others in the group.

Is self assessment really assessment? Perhaps it is one part of the reflective process that supports successful learning. By increasing self awareness of how and what is being learnt, we increase understanding of how to develop that learning. Self assessment can contribute to this process by providing markers of progress, perhaps including grades or quantitative measures that can be used as a score to show change over time. Reflections on experiences can contribute to the process of self assessment, allowing individuals to measure the ways in which they have changed or moved on as a result of their learning and evaluation of past experience.

Friends and colleagues as assessors

Traditionally, marking assignments has been seen as a key role for academic staff. Peer assessment allows the student to take on the tutor's role temporarily and learn from that experience. They learn by engaging in the assessment process and clarify their thinking by evaluating their peer's work and offering constructive feedback. It is important for the tutor to monitor this feedback so that no one is disadvantaged or hurt by the experience, but this also provides a learning opportunity as students develop skills in giving feedback and supporting other learners.

There are several ways in which online learning can be assessed by peers. Computer programs can receive assignments and distribute them to peers for marking. Usually in this kind of approach, students receive several assignments and in turn receive feedback from several of their peers. This increases the learning for the peer assessors who see several assignments and gives individuals a range of assessor comments. A more public approach can be used in workshops online. Students present their work in the form of a paper or a presentation and their peers give feedback and ask questions. A more personal approach can be to put students into small groups or pairs and ask them to share their assignments and discuss their findings. All these models are helped by clear guidelines and a checklist of criteria for the assignment. It can be particularly helpful if students are involved in the process of creating the checklist so that they commit to certain requirements.

The management of peer assessment is not always easy. There can be practical problems, such as individuals failing to mark assignments allocated to them. The emotional issues can also be problematic. Teachers usually have some training in giving feedback and have a sense of the impact of particular words on students. They are often committed to boosting the confidence of their learners in a way that fellow students may not be. The answer to these problems often lies in the approach used when setting up peer assessment. If members of a group 'buy into' the process and understand its value they are more likely to commit to working with others. It can also help if training is provided in giving feedback and some of the pitfalls are pointed out.

In the online learning environment peer assessment may be more problematic because of the lack of nonverbal clues to help participants to gauge how feedback is being received. There are also benefits in the online environment which support the peer assessment process. There is greater privacy for individuals meeting in breakout rooms than they might get in a physical classroom. Items that are to be reviewed by peers can be hidden from the main group. Preparation in breakout rooms is also a possible advantage. The example below highlights the value of peer assessment online.

> My students are doing a module about working with animals in the wild. It's difficult for them to get experience of different types of animals and their habitat, so for the assessment each student prepared a poster and a presentation to show what they had found out about one type of animal. During each presentation, others in the group had a scoring sheet for different aspects of the task and these were submitted anonymously for me to collate later and add my feedback. The students had taken photos, recorded interviews, made a collage of different food sources, enlarged pictures to show teeth and claws – the list goes on. It was an amazing display and they learned so much from assessing one another's presentation, giving credit for originality as well as factual information. We were transported to the great outdoors – it felt as if we'd spent a morning in the wild, not sitting at computers with headphones on!

Concerns have been raised about bias and the influence of friendship on peer assessors. This may be less of an issue online where relationships are more remote but the issue of considering the feelings of others is relevant to all peer assessors. One student gave the following account of her experience.

> I was very anxious about peer assessment. I'm not good at receiving feedback and I was fearful that I'd get upset or make a fool of myself. In fact, just the opposite happened. The tutor was really good. She made reference to peer assessment early on and then we worked together to create a list of things that we were looking for. We were put into pairs and given some time to talk about how we felt about the process of peer assessment. I was able to say how I felt and my partner was very respectful of my views and asked questions about what would work for me. Interestingly, she didn't feel the same way and almost seemed to welcome negative feedback – I thought she was very brave! Anyway, I think what happened was that she gave me the type of feedback I'd requested, and I did the same for her.

Research suggests that peer assessment is a valuable way of getting students involved in the learning process and although there can be issues about friendship and collusive marking, learners generally find the process fair and useful (Dochy et al., 1999).

The online facilitator as assessor

We have already considered many aspects of the online facilitator's role as an assessor. This includes creating assessment opportunities as part of the learning experience and supporting learners in self and peer assessment. Some of the case studies show the role of facilitators in observing participants and listening to their presentations and discussions.

The facilitator's role also involves engaging all learners by asking questions. The tools available in the virtual classroom can be particularly useful in getting answers to these questions. Here are some examples of questions and the way that web conferencing tools can be used to promote responses to the questions.

> "I want you to ask yourselves what this means for you. I'm going to set the timer for three minutes and I hope you'll be able to use that time to think about your answer."

> "Give me some examples from your experience. Use the hands up tool to let me know when you're ready to join in."

> "Let's consider the facts. What is the overall cost? I've put some suggestions on the screen. Use the voting tool to indicate which figure you think represents the overall cost."

> "Last time we considered some examples of our key theme. Can anyone remind us of any of these examples? Perhaps each of you could give me one example. I'll use the participant list and call on you each in turn starting at the top."

> "The exam questions will always ask you to analyse an issue that you have studied. What do we mean by the word analyse? Use the tool for typing text on the screen and add some words which could be part of a definition of the term 'analyse'."

These questions all have a different learning purpose. The facilitator is making connections with the learners' own thinking, their past experience, their past learning and their desire to be successful in a formal assessment. Questions pack a powerful punch in the learning game! Too many questions together undo the good work, so appropriate, well paced questioning stimulates the learners' thinking and prompts them to do some mental work by recalling something they already know or making connections with something familiar. Questions are particularly important in the online learning environment. They need to be delivered with care, so that learners use them as a learning cue. Here is an example of the use of questions in two different situations. What works here and what doesn't work so well? (You are being asked a question here which gives you a clue that the example may not be a positive one. It is also asking you to make judgements, another key use of questioning in the learning process.)

> This seminar is based on a series of questions. Who are the key players on the world stage? What influence do they have on global decision making? What is the impact of any global decisions? How do these decisions affect us at local level? Tell me what you think about these questions.

> I'm going to base this workshop on a series of questions. We'll take each one in turn and then try to make connections between the answers we have for each question and our overall theme. Workplace safety is big business. I wonder why that is? So the first question we need to answer is how did health and safety become a business in itself? What do you think? ... OK, so we've got a list of reasons why health and safety came to be a business priority. Let's consider next why it might be a priority in your own business. Why have you been asked to do this course? What are the safety issues in your area of work? ...

The answer to the question before these examples is very straightforward. The first example asks all the questions together and offers no chance to reflect on the questions individually. The facilitator asks a very big question at the end which probably leaves participants unsure how to answer. The second example uses questions more thoughtfully, giving time for participants to get into the subject in stages and linking the bigger questions with their own situation and motivation. In the same way that assessment may be used to structure the learning experience, so questions may be used to structure the presentation of key information.

If questioning is the cornerstone of learning, the next important thing to consider is how to involve learners in the questioning process. The key to this is the rapport and atmosphere of trust built up within the group by the facilitator. Questions can best be answered if there is a feeling of safety about expressing a view which may not be correct or acceptable. The rapport with learners and their willingness to answer questions is strengthened by the response from the facilitator to all responses. It can be easy to offer praise for a correct or useful answer but much more difficult to respond to an answer that is wrong or takes the discussion in a different direction. The role of the facilitator in assessment is to provide feedback which is honest and useful to the learner. The two terms may not always be compatible, particularly in an online learning situation where dialogue can be more difficult.

Giving positive feedback online requires thoughtful management. Firstly, it is helpful if any feedback is recorded so that learners have access to a written or audio account of what has been said, or at least bullet point notes of key points. Secondly, positive feedback should be as precise as any negative comments. Helping learners to understand what they do well, helps to prepare them for future assessments. It is easy to zoom in on the faults and forget that learners need to know what they do well so that they can repeat their success. The use of language is also very important, particularly when there is no nonverbal communication to support what is said. Many tutors and trainers have favourite words that they use again and again to praise good work or correct answers. These words range from 'brilliant' to 'fine' but usually mean the same thing. Greater precision is required online. It is helpful to identify words of praise that seem to fit the level of contribution. If a learner has delivered a presentation, giving thanks and appropriate words of praise are very important. If the learner has answered a brief question correctly, then perhaps a brief response is appropriate. The best feedback for learners is often a comment which has not been used before and is very specific to them. Personalising feedback gives a sense that the tutor or trainer is in touch with the learner and can make the assessment seem unique or special.

Giving negative feedback requires the same approach as for positive feedback, but it also requires that the learner is prepared to hear what is being said. It is very easy in an online situation for learners to 'tune out' and not listen to what is being said. It is like not opening a letter that contains bad news – if we leave the envelope sealed, there is no need to face up to the bad news it contains. One approach to engaging the learner is the praise sandwich. The tutor begins by praising something in the assessment, then offers the filling which is usually negative, and closes with the other slice of bread which is positive. This can be a good strategy, but it is also familiar to learners and they easily take the filling as the real focus for their attention and ignore the praise.

It is possibly more important to consider the context of the feedback before considering the content. It is helpful if there is some privacy for the participant receiving feedback. In the examples given earlier, if the feedback on the presentation was negative or the answer to the question was wrong, then the facilitator should try to avoid publicly highlighting errors. If there is an opportunity to give feedback in a breakout room or use an appointment system for learners to meet in a one to one situation, some goodwill may be established before tackling any problems by means of assessment. It can also be helpful if learners are given the task of identifying any problems. If they open the door to the discussion by talking about problems they see, this can make it much easier for the tutor or trainer to add to what has been said. If feedback is to be useful, the learner has to be receptive to what is being said – the tutor saying what is wrong with an assessment is not even half the process! Helping learners to receive feedback often means listening to what they have to say and using their comments to develop a dialogue which includes feedback. This can be very successful online, particularly if breakout rooms are used for privacy and learners feel able to speak freely.

IN SUMMARY

Assessment is not just about testing learning at the end of a course. In the online learning environment it can and should be an integral part of the learning experience. It can provide creative ways for learners to engage with a topic and the opportunity to collaborate with one another to increase their understanding.

- **Student centred learning and assessment** do go together very well. Assessment can be used to structure the learning experience and help to progressively build up knowledge and skills. This in turn helps learners to feel successful which motivates and encourages them.
- **Web conferencing for learning and assessment** offers unique opportunities to learners. The technology allows them to test their learning in many different ways. Other technology may be used to gather and store summative assessments so the role of the facilitator of live online learning is likely to include supporting learners to use this technology.
- **Students, peers and tutors** all have a role to play in the assessment process. Support for learners undertaking assessment is an essential part of the tutor's role, both practically and emotionally. Self and peer assessment offer online learners the opportunity to review their achievements in different ways.

9 Getting it right

The question, 'Am I getting it right?' can be quickly followed by another question, 'How would I know?' This chapter tries to answer both these questions by reviewing the skills required to be a facilitator of successful live online learning and ways of evaluating those skills. The image of a journey has been used several times in this book: this chapter considers the different stages in that journey towards becoming a confident and competent practitioner. It considers:

- early experiences of teaching in a virtual classroom
- making progress
- good practice
- stepping back
- personal reflections
- conversations with colleagues
- the learners' perspective
- the onward journey.

Early experiences of teaching in a virtual classroom

New teaching and learning situations can trigger feelings of excitement, but may also produce feelings of inadequacy about the ability to be a good teacher. Web conferencing challenges many tutors and trainers because it demands technical skills as well as subject knowledge. It also requires new approaches to teaching, perhaps taking us outside our comfort zone. Here are some reflections from tutors who found the online environment particularly challenging.

> Being timetabled to teach online was a bit of a shock. What was even more of a shock was that I just couldn't manage the technology. My teaching was so stilted because I was looking for the next button to press. Now I've been doing it for a couple of years, I read this and wonder what the fuss was about, but occasionally when things don't go quite right online the old panic comes back and I remember what it was like to be a learner with a capital L!

I found being an on online tutor really intense and quite exhausting. You have to attend to so many different things at once. You have to think about setting up the learning activities, paying attention to who's online, looking at the chat for feedback, or hands being raised with questions. As a classroom teacher one of the things you develop is a sense of having eyes at the back of your head, and it was a bit like that, but on a different basis, because it's all the windows on screen that you have to keep an eye on.

Research into the experiences of tutors who were new to web conferencing revealed similar insecurities. Tutors with a background in computing can be more confident about using the technology but still express concerns about managing the software as well as the learning experience.

In previous chapters, different aspects of the online learning experience are explored in detail. This chapter summarises key messages from these chapters in order to answer the question, 'Am I getting it right?' As usual, there are two aspects to this: developing the technical ability to manage the web conferencing system and the facilitation skills to manage the participants. The process begins with the facilitator becoming the learner.

Almost everyone who took part in our research stressed the need to experience online learning as a participant before becoming a facilitator. By doing this, they discovered the difficulties learners experienced, and also something about their personal likes and dislikes in the approaches taken by online facilitators. Often this first experience of being a learner was associated with training offered by the web conferencing provider for their institution. In some cases, individuals had taken part in a large online conference or webinar related to their subject area or online learning. This learning experience is described here by a new online tutor.

I joined an online session which was about webinars. The facilitator switched off our microphones, explaining that it would limit distractions from people coughing etc. I would have preferred to be trusted to switch my own microphone off! She spoke well, but she spoke for a long time and used slides with the same design, so that I wasn't sure where we were in the presentation. As a tutor, I'm more aware of all the things that bothered me as a participant – and I think very carefully about how my participants might react to what I do online.

One of the most valuable things that an apprentice online facilitator can do is to be an online learner and note what it feels like to be a learner. Even the most experienced online tutors and trainers say that they gain from the experience of being a participant in a variety of online settings.

The next stage of the learning process is to find out about the technology. For some new online tutors or trainers this may coincide with starting to teach online. Not everyone is given the luxury of a training period before being asked to use web conferencing to deliver a course. It is also true that some of the tools used in web conferencing can only really be experienced when participants are online together. In Chapter 2, we reviewed the basics of using a web conferencing system. Here is a summary of key points for getting started with web conferencing.

- There will be a procedure for getting participants together online. This can either be through a link sent to them, or a registration system which allows them access.
- The facilitator will need moderator privileges to allow access to all the tools. Materials will have to be prepared for the online session, either through presentation software or using the web conferencing tools.
- When everyone is online, they need to be able to switch on the microphone, use the chat tool, the emoticons, the step away tool and perhaps some of the whiteboard tools for annotation. The moderator will need to be able to move the slides on if there is a presentation, or use new whiteboard screens, and also observe messages and 'hands up' signs indicating that participants want some attention.
- The moderator needs to be able to 'read' the screen, to see who is online and on the participant list, and also if they step away or appear to lose their internet connection.
- Participants are likely to use the chat box, so decisions have to be made about what posts are visible to other participants or just to the moderator.
- If participants have used interaction tools such as the 'hands up' tool or the emoticons, the moderator must know how to switch them off.
- Finally, it is important to know how to make recordings and save resources such as the whiteboards at the end of the session.

Much more could be added, but if the technical side becomes too complicated, it can be harder to focus on the learning needs of the participants. A new online tutor describes this experience.

> I found the multi-tasking very stressful. I would start speaking and my microphone wouldn't be on. I'd write something in the chat box and I'd realise I hadn't sent it to the group, or I hadn't noticed that someone had their hand up, or else I'd noticed that their hand was up but then I'd completely forgotten to respond and was chattering on about something else. It was a real challenge for me to do all of that seamlessly. I was in an unfamiliar setting where I was beginning to be aware that I wasn't doing the social stuff as well as I would have liked to, because my brain was trying to cope with, 'Have I switched this on?' 'Is this working?' 'Can they hear me?'

This example clearly shows the dual role of the tutor or trainer online in managing the tools and facilitating the learning. The tutor refers to the need to do the 'social stuff'. This often comes quite naturally in a normal classroom, but online can feel very stilted. The following facilitator skills are very important, particularly when getting to know participants online.

- There is a need to imagine how the session will begin, even before the official start time, so that the facilitator has planned how to greet individuals and what sort of 'chat' will be used to build rapport and help participants to feel at ease.
- An awareness of the level of support the group will need when using the technology is essential, and low key reminders and offers of help should be included in the plan for the session.
- It can also be helpful to prepare the participants for what will happen in the workshop, perhaps using a prepared agenda, and remind them regularly of progress through the agenda and relevant timings for breaks or activities. This may sound like stating the obvious, but in our research, experienced tutors suggested that they needed to be more aware of timing online and more careful about sticking to a schedule than they were in a physical classroom.
- We have made reference several times in previous chapters to the need to speak kindly to participants, giving them a sense that the facilitator is aware of their needs and keen to be supportive. Acknowledging that it may not be easy to do something initially can help to put participants at ease.
- Again, it may sound obvious to suggest that facilitators should listen to the participants carefully and make them feel comfortable about speaking to the group by valuing their contributions. However familiar this kind of

instruction seems, online it might not feel quite so easy. Prepare the phrases you might use in advance, so that you have actually thought about how the words will sound.

- In a learner centred approach, it is important that the facilitator avoids talking about herself too much. If she is struggling with the technology or this is the first session online with a group, it might be better not to make a big deal of it. A simple apology, or 'oops, pressed the wrong button', is as much as participants need to hear.

Perhaps, the online presence we are describing here is a tutor or trainer on their best behaviour! In Chapter 6, we talked about one tutor possibly seeming too caring but warned against too much 'bite' in the online dialogue. The participants' expressions are not visible so there are few clues to tell if they are unhappy with anything that has been said, so the facilitator has to think carefully about how comments might be received by the group. Similarly, if participants are too outspoken or say too much, it is helpful to have some comments ready to soothe the situation and move on. Here are some examples – do they please or antagonise?

> “OK, I'm the boss here and my decision is that we move on now.”

> “People usually get this wrong so I suppose I'd better tell you yet again what you have to do.”

> “That was a really helpful story. Let's just summarise the ideas we've had so far.”

> “We're going to stop for a 10 minute break now. I'll set the timer and perhaps you could just press the button to show that you've stepped away.”

> “Oh, my goodness, I'm so sorry. I thought I'd pressed the button for the timer but obviously not. It's so stressful trying to teach and work the technology. I feel such a disaster when I get it wrong. I do apologise.”

> “Maybe just talk among yourselves while I try to sort this out.”

By now you will be able to select for yourself which of these comments is most likely to engage learners and which is most likely to enrage them.

This section has been about early experiences of working in the virtual classroom. It has referred to points made earlier in the book and offered a review of the key skills for online facilitators. This also provides a starting point for considering how these skills can be developed.

▶ Making progress

Planning online sessions is essential from the beginning for all online tutors or trainers. As tutors and trainers become more experienced, planning becomes even more critical. As more complex uses of the technology are introduced and more is asked of participants, it is essential to choreograph the learning experience very carefully. The design of a lesson plan, and the level of detail it contains, is often chosen to suit individual preferences, or to meet institutional requirements, or to suit the delivery method. The essential components of an online session plan are likely to be:

- information about the session, such as the name of the group or the subject and the time
- aims and learning outcomes
- resources
- an agenda
- each activity in the session, including:
  - timing
  - details of the activity, including what the facilitator and participants have to do
  - tools and resources, including any technical instructions for you, or reminders for participants
  - possible use of language at different points in the process
  - reminders for the end of the session
  - reflection/evaluation
- reminders of tasks to be completed after the online session.

Preparing an online session should include planning the way that participants will be encouraged to take part, particularly if activities are introduced that require them to reflect on personal experiences or share their thoughts with others. There is also a need to plan an escape route if individuals get into difficulty or speak for too long about something that is too personal or irrelevant to the rest of the group. Here is an example of the script used by one online tutor.

The next activity is about your experiences of caring for others. The caring role is one that is familiar to most people, even if they're not involved in the care profession like you. Even caring for a pet gives us some idea of what it's like to put the needs of others before our own. In your assessment, you'll be asked to write a case study of a caring experience. I'll give you much more detail of this later on – and lots of help in preparing it – but for today I want us to explore the topic by reflecting on different experiences of caring. By sharing our experiences, hopefully, we'll all learn about a range of different caring roles. It can be difficult to speak about your own experiences, particularly if they've been sad or involved the loss of someone you loved, so choose your example carefully so that it's something that you can speak about without becoming upset. I hope no one is panicking about being asked to do this – there is an option to stay silent. I'll go over my plan for this activity and then ask for any questions. The slide shows how it's going to work, giving the timings and the groups. First, we'll take some time to prepare individually. During this time, anyone who would prefer to remain silent can let me know using the chat option which only I can read. Then we'll go into groups and share experiences and finally, a spokesperson for each group will tell the whole group some of the highlights of the experiences described and the discussion about them.

This tutor has carefully considered how participants might feel and has provided them with safeguards, such as not taking part or choosing an example that they can talk about without distress. The introduction to this activity is quite long, and it feels as if the tutor is giving the participants time to get used to the idea of telling their own story. He makes reference to possible motivating factors, such as being part of a profession and the assessment they will have to complete. He offers reassurance and tries to build their confidence by showing understanding. Finally, he provides a slide and a spoken account explaining how the activity will be organised. Many online activities require much less introduction than this, but here we have a good example of thoughtful planning when a sensitive topic is involved. In a classroom situation, many of the remarks made by this tutor would be made in response to the looks on the faces of individuals or to queries from them. Online participants may not speak out so readily to ask questions, and fears and anxieties cannot be picked up from body language or facial expressions.

The example above also requires a plan for getting participants into groups and appointing a spokesperson. When participants are asked to go into breakout rooms to discuss a given topic, it may be important to identify roles such as chairperson or spokesperson when returning to the main room. As participants are not able to see one another and may not always be familiar with others in the group, it is important to handle role allocation sensitively. Asking for volunteers is a good approach. Similarly, agreeing with the group that everyone will take it in turns to facilitate the work in breakout rooms can be very helpful. Perhaps the most important thing is to give participants a get-out clause, so that without embarrassment they can say 'pass' if they feel unable to take a leading role. In the virtual classroom, leaving participants to sort themselves out can lead to long silences and a lot of confusion.

This section was headed 'Making progress' because it refers to the stage when online facilitators can use their knowledge of web conferencing facilities and online learners' needs to plan and prepare live online sessions which are more complex. Good practice is about taking this a step further, so that live online sessions have a seamless quality, but also have more flexibility because the facilitator is confident about making unplanned changes.

Good practice

Success for most tutors and trainers is a work in progress and subject to many variables, but there is a sense of aspiration in the role – a desire for best practice.

Technical competence and confidence are an important part of the profile for a successful online facilitator. However, there is still a need to regularly refresh our knowledge of what the system can do. It is important not to use tools just because they are there, but equally we need to use the best tool for our purpose. Making choices for learning online implies knowing what is available. It is also important to be aware of new developments that will help the learning process.

Good practice is also about the skills involved in supporting online learners. Here is an account from a tutor who sees the progression she has made in supporting learners as well as managing the technology.

> For me it was a process of going back to my experience as a new teacher. What I discovered when I got into the online environment was that there were all sorts of things that I knew how to do instinctively if I was faced with a group, that I hadn't worked out how to do with online learners. If someone is coming in the door of the classroom, you say 'hello', or you

say 'how are you today?' and you notice whether they're looking worried or upbeat. All these things that I'd completely forgotten were central to the way I work with groups, suddenly flashed back up as real issues for me, because I wasn't sure how to do it in the online environment.

I realised that I needed to be a bit less intuitive and a bit more ordered about the use of time. The intensity of the sessions requires very clear planning. You have to pay attention to what you're trying to do, how long you've got for each activity, how you're going to move people in and out of rooms, how long it will take, where are they going to get the information they need, have you prepared them enough for what they have to do.

This account of the experience of good practice as an online tutor highlights the need to develop different skills to support online learners, particularly careful planning and timing. She describes herself as having regressed to the way she felt when she first started teaching. There is also a reminder of the need to manage the learning experience and the technology in an integrated way.

The development of professional competence in the virtual classroom allows us to manage a range of experiences confidently, making changes to our plan in a responsive and pragmatic way, without disrupting the learning process and frequently enhancing it. Here is an example of this responsive approach.

I realised that the discussion was slow in the main group and that it would be better to have smaller groups in breakout rooms. It was very satisfying to have the technical fluency and confidence in my judgement to quickly set up breakout rooms and suggest a new approach to the group.

Like the tutor in the example above, the intuitive practitioner is able to sense a need in a learning situation and address it comfortably. In the online learning environment there is often so much going on that the facilitator struggles to process all the available feedback from learners and groups. Evidence of real progress for the online tutor or trainer is a sense that they have become an intuitive practitioner who is more at ease with the technology and can see and hear more as a result – a bit like driving and listening to the radio at the same time, as we process the road signs and what other drivers are doing but also engage with the radio programme. There is no sense of complacency, but rather the feeling that more is now possible. It is safe to depart from the prepared script if that meets learner needs. It is possible to use tools that are just right for the moment without preparation or practice, because we feel confident that all will be well. Compare this feeling with the descriptions given by tutors earlier in the book and this gives a sense of real progression.

Although this sense of moving on is about confidence it is also about successful implementation of a wide range of strategies that are known to support online learning. At the top of this list is the need to prepare online learners for the experience, both in terms of knowing their way round the system and understanding how to make use of the learning opportunities on offer. Planning and preparation of online sessions is essential. This planning includes planning how to use language most effectively and considering a range of responses to content and activities. It is important to get the timing of an online session right and to provide instructions so that participants know what to expect and what they are being asked to do. Variety and stimulating content make a real difference to learner engagement – the phrase 'drift away' is used in a later example to describe the feeling of losing touch with the content of an online presentation. Being responsive during a workshop to all the different clues provided by participants about their reaction to the learning experience is important too. Additionally we need to check that what we think is happening is what is actually happening, both in terms of technical issues and the learners' understanding of the topic.

▶ Stepping back

We have considered the different ways in which we develop expertise in managing web conferencing technology and supporting learners online. However, throughout the online apprenticeship and beyond there is a need to acknowledge that competence and confidence are easily undermined. This is a common experience when software is updated or systems are replaced with something new. Even simple changes like an icon being in a different place can disrupt the 'flow' that has been evidence of success before the change took place. New groups, new technology, a break from online tutoring, or a personal issue that affects our well being and confidence, can all impact on our status as successful practitioners. It can feel as if we have taken a backward step. Two experienced tutors give their view of stepping back.

> When you're using new technologies there will always be a going back – there will always be a loop back to that early stage when you were unsure what to do, until you figure out how you can maximise the potential of the new.

> There are overlaps from one stage to another stage in learning to be a good online facilitator, but definitely repeats and stepping back. At some point you're going to drop back to feeling as if you've only got a basic grasp of the new tools and new technologies, until you become comfortable again and look at enhancing your practice once more.

Both of these examples suggest that there is an opportunity in the experience of feeling as if we have gone backwards in our learning. Finding that opportunity may be about getting some help with the technology, but also about our own reflective practice and seeking feedback from others about their experiences in the virtual classroom.

▶ Personal reflections

What do you say when you talk to yourself? Most of us have an inner dialogue about teaching experiences which reviews our role and interaction with our learners. Being busy at work can often mean that this inner dialogue is most apparent when we are having difficulty getting to sleep at night or driving home from work. It is also influenced by our mood, energy levels, self esteem and personality traits, so that we see experiences in a more positive or negative light. This inner dialogue is not really reflective practice but does have an impact on how we evaluate our role as an online facilitator. Reflective practice usually involves written or verbal commentary on what happened in our teaching practice, analysis of why it happened and perhaps some thoughts about how things might be done differently. Does reflective practice help you to understand what has happened in a learning session and positively consider what worked well and what needs to be different? Or does reflective practice easily become a negative inner dialogue which leaves you feeling insecure and unsure about what you should do?

The evidence from reflective journals kept by new online facilitators suggests that there is a tendency to focus on what has gone wrong, particularly technical issues which are often temporary. Here are examples from two reflective journals, one supporting the view that reflections after an online session can focus on negatives, and the other suggesting that it is a helpful record of what happened and how things might be improved in future.

Tutor 1: Made so many mistakes today. I couldn't add to the text on the whiteboard, so every time I typed a comment I created a new text box. I wanted to leave one of the breakout rooms and ended up dragging the whole group back into the main room. I kept forgetting to switch my microphone on and I'd be speaking away and no one could hear. The list goes on, but the worst thing was the panic – my competence seemed to disappear. Even things that I normally do easily, I suddenly seemed unsure about.

Tutor 2: The activities with photos worked fine – groups talked well amongst themselves and brought back some interesting points to the plenary. Issues like race and gender were discussed in depth in a way that I've never heard them discussed in a face to face workshop. I wonder if that is a reflection of the supposed security that being online and invisible affords. In the presentation after the break I couldn't get the pointer to work and afterwards realised that I was trying to point with clipart – duhhh! I lost track of time a bit whilst presenting. Maybe I should use the timer on my phone.

Both tutors were working online with another tutor so it was possible to get a different perspective on what happened. The co-tutor with Tutor 1 agreed that there appeared to be some loss of confidence about halfway through but said that before that the tutor was doing really well, particularly when involving the participants in activities and encouraging them to talk to one another. Tutor 2 sounds much more positive and much calmer about making a mistake. She is able to highlight positive experiences and acknowledge what went well and what could be done differently in the future. These examples highlight the tendency to be selective in analysing a teaching session. An online facility which may enhance the reflective process is the ability to record sessions. Using video recordings to support reflective practice suggests that seeing a session is more valuable than just remembering it.

Reflective practice is one of the tools that professionals in different disciplines can make use of to help them to analyse their choices at work and develop their understanding of issues and experiences. It can be further developed by considering the views of others and the way in which different perspectives inform our understanding of any experience. Brookfield (2006) describes his theory of the four lenses, looking at the learning experience from four different perspectives:

the teacher's experience, the learner's experience, colleagues' viewpoints and those of educational theorists. In business, appraisal of performance can be carried out using a 360 degree model (Lepsinger and Lucia, 2009) looking at an individual's performance from the perspective of customers, managers, colleagues and the employee who is being appraised. These models of evaluation imply a holistic view of an experience. To evaluate our teaching experience online, we can use both reflective practice and conversations with others to help us to explore and clarify what has been achieved.

Conversations with colleagues

Canning (2008) makes the case against relying on personal reflection alone, which he sees as often characterised by familiar interpretations of experiences rather than new insights. He believes that the expert teacher is willing to share experiences with colleagues as part of a collective learning experience. Commentary from online tutors suggests that they often feel insecure about their practice and that conversations with others help them to feel less negative about experiences online and offer them useful opportunities to share knowledge and skills. Conversations with colleagues also offer a creative opportunity which most online tutors value. The case studies in this book have offered a taste of these conversations, allowing a glimpse of the experiences of other online tutors, sharing perspectives, challenges and solutions.

Reflective practice is a powerful tool when used wisely. Immediately after a workshop we may feel exhausted or deflated, or in contrast quite 'high', but these feelings are not always the most useful ones to record. The most valuable reflections come when the emotions are calmer and analysis is more balanced. Add to these the perspective offered by colleagues, and the true reflection begins to emerge. The picture becomes more complete when the evaluation of the learners is added to the mix. The experience we have reflected on so personally is reflected back to us by others and located in a bigger picture of a shared experience.

The learners' perspective

The learners' evaluation of the online experience is a particularly valuable resource. It allows our learners to teach us how to be as good as we can be online. The feedback we referred to in Chapter 6 is part of the evaluation of what is happening in real time online and helps us to make adjustments to suit learner needs. This immediate responsiveness is essential but it is also important to gain an objective overview of what learners have gained from an online session. As with so many aspects of online teaching and learning, the evaluation strategies used in the normal classroom are not always as useful online.

Deciding how to evaluate learning, requires that we first decide what we want to know about the learning experience. Here is an example from the tutor of the social care group who was asking participants to give examples of their own experiences of caring for others.

Evaluation of session on caring experiences

Purpose:

- to evaluate the range of learning from this activity
- to evaluate the approach used in terms of participants' comfort level and ability to take part
- to evaluate tutor approach, including use of language, support, timing, type of examples given by the tutor.

Strategies:

- questioning and checking during session, noting any issues
- recording the number of times each participant contributed and any reluctance to take part during main group activity
- recording the number of questions asked by participants and their contributions in small groups
- asking participants to complete Post It style boxes anonymously, on the whiteboard giving an example of something important they had heard during the session
- sending a follow up email to all participants asking them to reply with an evaluation of the session.

This may seem like a lot of evaluation, and it would not be practical for every group or every activity. Learners also become weary of being asked to give feedback. In this case, it seems likely that they would value the opportunity to give their opinion on a very personal learning experience which involved some risk for the learners.

More objective evaluation systems often involve quantitative data and ask participants to give a grade or score to represent their opinion of a learning experience. Scoring systems give a useful overview of learning preferences and can be used to gather institutional statistics on learner satisfaction. However, the scores given rarely help us to understand the learners' experiences and this is essential for the online tutor. If a participant gives an unsatisfactory score or selects 'poor' rather than 'very good' we have no way of knowing if there was a technical problem or if the learning experience failed to meet their expectations.

The more specific the evaluation is, the more likely it is that we will learn from our learners. This brings us back to the purpose of the evaluation. In the example given earlier, the purpose was to find out about a specific activity. In the following example, participants were asked to put comments into the chat box after they had listened to a presentation from an expert in their field. The presentation was recorded, not live. The presenter's voice could be heard and his slides were shown on the whiteboard. Initials have been used to indicate different participants' messages in the web conferencing chat box.

CHAT

J: listening on line was pretty easy. I think it's helpful to have something to look at by way of slides and other stuff on the screen, without them it may be easy to have your eyes (and brain) wander to something interesting happening around you

D: Quite difficult at the start to concentrate on listening and try and take notes at same time …

A: To be honest I wasn't too keen. I found it much more difficult to concentrate on a disembodied voice. The sound quality is also very distracting.

D: It was fine but I found that due to the feeling of distance from the lecture I have to really focus and not get distracted by other things.

H: It is more difficult as you don't have hand gestures or body language to help you

I: I found myself starting to drift away a little, so going to have to keep myself in check

C: I found it absolutely fine. Presentation was very clear and easily understood. Visual slides helped, and there was lots of checking that we had understood before moving on to next part.

Seven out of ten participants gave feedback in the chat box. There were different opinions about the value of the presentation, but overall it seems that this was not the easiest way for learners to work online and might be better presented in a different way or using an alternative resource. Brookfield (2006) talks about 'hunting assumptions' when evaluating student learning. In this example, it would be easy to assume that the presentation, which had been a big success when delivered to a group in a classroom, might be equally useful online, but this was not the case.

A frequent problem with online evaluation is lack of response from participants. This may mean that the evaluation needs to be more subtle or included in a fairly natural way in an online session. Feedback at the end of a session or sent by email is more likely to be given less attention because the participants are tired, or busy, or moving on to something else. Evaluation, like feedback, needs to be included in the lesson plan and possibly scripted to ensure that it is presented in a way that motivates learners to take part. It is also important to select evaluation methods that are likely to appeal to a specific group of learners. The digital age means that visual, fast paced activities are more likely to get the attention of learners than long, wordy questionnaires. A tutor who had a group of young learners online wanted to know if they liked his chosen learning

Figure 9.1 Example of visual evaluation of learning activities using emoticons

approaches so he created a slide with a picture representing each of the activities, such as group work (Figure 9.1), a film clip, a quiz. He asked the participants to use the emoticons to show how they felt about each activity. He then produced a score sheet at the end of each session for the different activities and asked the learners to confirm that the activities that scored highest were really the most useful for learning. He attempted to make use of their feedback in subsequent sessions and checked that they continued to give similar responses. If not, he changed his approach to fit their feedback. This is about responsiveness within limits, rather than revising a whole course, but participants in this case would feel that their feedback had value because it led to a change in approach.

Participants can also give visual feedback in response to statements about their learning, as in Figure 9.2.

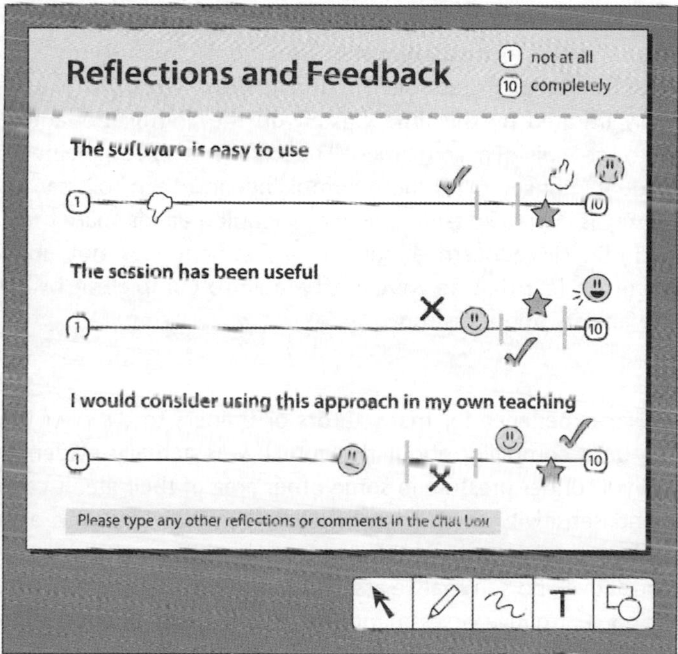

Figure 9.2 Example of evaluation of learning activities using clip art

Another important purpose of evaluation is to find out the long term impact of learning resulting from online learning experiences. Impact is high on the agenda of quality initiatives in many educational institutions. For some learners impact is about increased awareness which is very difficult to measure, whereas for others it might be about employability or passing an assessment.

Evaluating the impact of online learning may be undertaken as part of a formal, institution-wide process, but for individual online facilitators evaluating impact is also about finding out if the learning experience is meeting the objectives of individual learners. It is particularly important to find ways to give different individuals a voice in commenting on their learning experience so that the one or two loud voices in a group feedback situation are not allowed to dominate our perception. Some participants choose not to make a public comment but may not agree with those who do. Students who complain about a course or assessment may be perfectly justified in their comments, but they may also have another agenda that is not known to their tutor and other participants. Here is an example provided by an online tutor.

> One of my students took every opportunity to complain about the assessment task. I felt as if I was being rude when I tried to move the session on. No one else spoke so I assumed that they agreed with him. Individual conversations at a later date told a different story. The other participants were really irritated by the time wasted on the complaints and by my niceness to the individual concerned! The student who complained began his individual interview with more complaints and then told me that his young son was ill in hospital and he was spending all his spare time at his son's bedside. His concern about the assessment was not about the content but his fear that he wouldn't be able to complete it by the due date, and anxiety about his son.

It is a familiar experience for many tutors or trainers to discover that what seemed to be a complaint about the course was actually evidence that a participant was under pressure in some other area of their life. It can require patience and sensitivity to discover whether the individual has a personal issue or if the complaints about the course are valid.

Both formative and summative assessments allow us to measure and evaluate learning. Formative assessment can give a great deal of information about what learning is taking place. In other chapters in this book, we have considered a range of strategies for checking learning. A common example is the use of a quiz which can be fun, can help learners to recall information, and can give us feedback on learning that has taken place, but in the context of evaluation, it can also help us to work out what teaching and learning strategies are most helpful for our learners.

Summative assessment may involve external examination of learners' work or tutors themselves may be involved in carrying out the assessment.

Whichever is the case, there is an opportunity to measure the success of learners. There is a need to treat results with caution, because they depend on what is being tested and how assessments are marked. In terms of evaluating whether we have achieved the agreed aims of a particular course and helped our learners to achieve their goals, the results of summative assessments may seem like the ultimate evaluation of our skills as a teacher.

Evaluation is about checking the participants' view of teaching and learning. In the online learning environment, a vacuum quickly appears unless we know how learners are responding. The visible signs of a positive learning experience, such as shared good humour or seeing groups enjoying working together, are missing online. There may be a tendency for tutors and trainers to be over critical of themselves, thinking that they could do better. The participants' responses in an evaluation can give reassurance and increase understanding of what works well and anything that could be done differently.

▶ The onward journey

Teaching and learning online can feel like uncharted territory. The purpose of this chapter is to offer reassurance that there are known components of successful online teaching and learning, based on experience and research. Additionally, we can use different methods of evaluation to increase our understanding of our progress as online facilitators.

The final chapter of this book considers the onward journey for facilitators of live online learning. It shows that web conferencing offers unique opportunities to include learners in learning experiences that have not been available to them before. The themes of creativity and learner centred approaches are developed as we consider innovative ways to use the technology. Getting it right is also about this onward journey, embracing innovation and new opportunities for learning.

IN SUMMARY

The components of successful online teaching and learning

- Getting it right is a subjective construct, but there are ways of checking that we are getting it right for our learners and that we are progressing as facilitators of online learning.

- Taking part in online learning sessions allows us to experience being a learner and to note what that feels like.
- Developing technical skills for online delivery is a phased process, including returning to a state of 'not knowing' when technology changes.
- Managing the learning experience for online learners is different from facilitating learning face to face and requires different skills and new insights.
- Planning and preparation needs to be detailed and focused on the online experience. It may include imagining how individual participants might respond to a particular task or use of language. Preparing the words we intend to use to encourage and motivate learners may also be helpful.
- Preparing the learner for the online experience is particularly important. This includes providing written and spoken instructions which make it clear what learners have to do.
- Including feedback strategies in our planning is essential.

Self evaluation

- Reflective practice is an important part of the evaluation of the work we do online. It should highlight successes and progress in our journey as online facilitators, as well as directing us to new ways of working.
- Reflective practice is part of the evaluation process, but conversations with colleagues and others who work online are also important, providing opportunities for others to reflect on our experiences and for us to gain new ideas.

Evaluation by others

- The preparation of online learning sessions should include strategies for getting feedback from participants.
- Negative self evaluation or negative comments from an individual may lead us to make false judgments about our performance or choice of activities. It is important to canvas all views so that silence online is not judged inaccurately. Listening to learners' feedback and encouraging all learners to offer comment provides a balanced view of the learning experience.

- Both informal and formal systems of evaluation are valuable. The use of brief comments on screen, chat box messages, or small group discussions in breakout rooms can offer specific feedback that can be missing in a more formal overview of a course.
- Teachers may shy away from evaluation, but taking the opportunity to check their choices and approaches online may offer reassurance and guidance that cannot be found elsewhere.

10 Creative and inclusive live online learning

Throughout this book we have considered creative and innovative approaches to live online learning. A wide range of activities that can be undertaken in a virtual classroom have been covered, but there are still many other ways in which the technology can be used to support learning. This chapter provides examples of creative and inclusive ways of using web conferencing technology to support diverse groups of learners, to bring online and face to face learners together, and to help blend different tools and approaches. The chapter covers:

- creating an inclusive learning space
- innovative approaches to using web conferencing
- exploring the potential of web conferencing technology.

Creating an inclusive learning space

Web conferencing can provide an accessible and inclusive environment for learning. The opportunities provided by the range of media allow a wide variety of learner needs to be accommodated, as illustrated in earlier chapters. However, special preparation and thought may be needed when dealing with some groups of learners, for instance those from diverse cultural or geographical backgrounds and with specific individual learning needs. Consideration of live online learning with these groups demonstrates that measures taken to address their needs will help create an effective learning space that will benefit all learners.

International learners

Meeting the needs of international learners and providing opportunities for working in a global context is part of the strategy of most educational institutions. Working with international students, whether they are spread across time zones or located together but from diverse cultural backgrounds, creates interesting challenges for a teacher or trainer. These include logistical issues such as timing of sessions, using appropriate learner centred strategies, and supporting those whose first language is not the same as the language of the course.

Finding appropriate times to meet geographically dispersed learners requires compromise. A tutor working with learners on the other side of the world may have to be online well outside their normal office hours. Even relatively small time differences within a group can create problems. A tutor working with learners across a range of countries in the Arabian Peninsula wanted to respond to her learners' request to take breaks in line with prayer times. However, since learners were located across a range of time zones, prayer times also varied, and made this impossible. Difficulties finding convenient times for online sessions can also be faced when trying to gather together a range of work based learners, since they will be balancing diverse professional and family commitments alongside their learning. A facilitator may not be able to address the challenges faced by learners so that they can engage in live online learning at a particular time, but they can ensure that sessions are used effectively and productively for tasks and activities that could not be done in any other way.

Another challenge for some international students is the active learner centred approach that works best in web conferencing sessions. Many cultures have a long history of teacher led approaches to education, in which teachers are given tremendous respect as unquestionable experts. To help learners from cultures where debate and discussion are uncommon to participate fully in a learner centred environment requires carefully designed activities which gradually build confidence and skills. Strategies which encourage appropriate contributions, academic discussion and critical thinking benefit all learners and can be built into to a course without singling out individuals. Bligh (2000) advises those who use discussion in their teaching to begin with simple, short tasks for small groups, then gradually increase the complexity, size and duration of tasks. This advice is also appropriate for virtual classroom activities and can support a gradual shift from teacher led to learner centred approaches. Setting expectations from the beginning of a course, as discussed in Chapter 2, will also help to establish ground rules and learners' roles and responsibilities.

Groups in which there are a variety of first languages can be challenging to facilitate. The lack of visual feedback and the reticence that learners may have to raise questions make it difficult for a facilitator to know when individuals are struggling because of language issues. Learners may feel embarrassed about admitting to difficulties in front of a group of peers, or lack the language skills to express anxieties. In a classroom context it is common for a learner to feel more comfortable admitting problems to another student rather than asking the tutor directly, and using the various media it is possible to encourage this in a virtual classroom. All learners can be advised to use the chat tool to request repetition or clarification of new words and ideas, and the facilitator can ensure that they type new terminology or complex vocabulary into the chat box to clarify spellings. If a second facilitator is available they could deal with the text conversation, but peers can also be encouraged to contribute key words, definitions and explanations. This approach offers a useful opportunity for the facilitator to assess wider understanding of content. The transcript of a text chat can usually be saved, so those who need help can refer to this later in private. Since these strategies will benefit anyone new to the vocabulary or conceptual ideas of a subject area it is, once again, not necessary to single out those with difficulties as the focus.

Another strategy which benefits all learners is to suggest the use of tools that indicate whether the speaker is going too slowly or too quickly. Whilst those with language difficulties appreciate this, so too does anyone with audio problems, and the strategy can be presented as a way of evaluating the facilitator's style rather than as an indicator of learner difficulties. As this facilitator recognises, responding to the request to speak a little more slowly, and remembering to remain at an appropriate pace, is a different matter altogether and can be a significant challenge in amongst all the other demands of the virtual classroom.

> I knew one of the group spoke Spanish but I didn't know how good his English was. The rest of the group were very confident contributors so the session was fast paced and I worried it might be difficult for the Spanish speaker. I tried to slow down my own rate of speaking and the pace of the activities, but things soon speeded up again. I felt awful when one of the participants said to me 'you know that Juan is from Mexico?', clearly as a reminder that he would be finding the session very difficult. It was very hard to accommodate the different language abilities and I would take more care with the structure of the session next time. I would provide opportunities for working in smaller groups so that Juan could speak with peers rather than feeling pressurised to contribute to or keep up with the whole group discussion.

This example highlights some of the themes that have emerged throughout this book: the importance of knowing and understanding learners' characteristics and needs, the need for appropriate planning and preparation, and the value of a flexible learner centred approach to facilitation. The use of strategies which prioritise learner interaction and group discussion over tutor led large group dialogue also ensures that everyone is included in a supportive learning environment.

Working with diversity

Some of the strategies for using the range of media available to help those with language issues can be adapted to suit other individuals. Someone with a speech impairment, or even a sore throat, may prefer text interaction rather than audio. On the other hand someone with a physical disability or a wrist injury might prefer to avoid typing and make contributions using audio. Where particular needs are known these can be accommodated and activities designed to provide equitable experiences. However, issues that impact on learners' ability to contribute in particular ways are not always known, and may arise without warning, as in the example given earlier of a learner who did not want to speak during a session as a result of personal issues. Decisions about which media are most appropriate may need to be made during a session. For the facilitator this requires a degree of confidence with the tools and a willingness to be flexible about facilitation strategies and planned activities. Issues such as group composition for breakout room activities may also have to be approached creatively to meet all learners' needs. For instance one group in which everyone will use audio and one where everyone will use text could be created, or mixed media use could be encouraged in all groups.

Accessibility tools built into web conferencing software support a wide range of learner needs and it is important to understand how to do things such as change font size, colour or screen layout, or provide audio notification of tool use. Other steps that can be taken to meet learners' needs include using breakout rooms where one to one support is needed, or to provide a space for private conversations if learners are reticent about expressing difficulties or preferences in front of a larger group. As in any learning scenario it may be helpful to provide access to reading materials or activity instructions in advance to allow those with sight or cognitive difficulties to arrive at a session adequately prepared. Strategies that support learners with particular needs should be considered in the virtual classroom as in any other setting.

At our own training sessions for potential facilitators, some tutors and trainers who see the potential of web conferencing, nevertheless state emphatically that 'it won't work for my learners' because of their particular characteristics or needs. Those who work with younger learners may feel that there are opportunities for learners to disrupt proceedings by using tools inappropriately or by creating spurious technical excuses for non-participation. However, web conferencing has been successfully used with younger learners. In Canada, for example, where distance education is a feature of K-12 public education, some provinces and growing numbers of schools are making use of synchronous online learning tools including web conferencing (Bennett, 2012).

The concerns of tutors and trainers who work with older learners often centre on the technical ability of participants. However, older learners are as diverse as any other section of the population and our experiences suggest that confidence with technology is more important than age. Less confident learners may take more time than others to adapt to the multimodal nature of the environment, and initially express reluctance or discomfort when faced with the complete range of tools. Using an approach in which a limited range of features are used during an activity (perhaps whiteboard and audio without chat), rather than asking participants to follow audio, text, whiteboard and web cams all at once, is helpful for everyone. Recordings may be particularly useful and allow reassurance to be given that not everything has to be remembered at once. Finding creative ways to encourage diverse learners to collaborate with live online learning can help to facilitate communication between people who would not otherwise interact.

The examples above illustrate that an inclusive learning environment can be created using web conferencing without singling out particular groups or individuals. Developing learners' skills for the virtual classroom by gradually introducing different tools, building up from simple activities to more complex ones, and providing options for interaction benefits everyone and facilitates meaningful learning.

Innovative applications of web conferencing

Live online learning provides an opportunity to create innovative learning experiences which bring together:

- **learners and resources** – a wide range of online resources, and resources that learners have available in their own context, can be used to support learning in a virtual classroom
- **learners and experts** – remote experts or specialists who would not otherwise be accessible can be brought into a virtual classroom
- **local and remote learners** – web conferencing allows interaction between learners in a classroom and other learners in different locations
- **different online approaches** – live online learning can be mixed with other online approaches to create opportunities for new activities and course designs.

Learners and resources

The case against online learning is often that it cannot be used for practical activities. Whilst it may be true that you should not learn to drive a car or perform heart surgery without some hands-on experience, with a bit of creativity many practical activities can be adapted for an online classroom. Chapter 4 included an example where learners were asked to bring along props for an online session on nursing, then used these to complete practical activities. Chapter 3 included introductory activities using a picture of a 'tray of objects', adapted from a face to face activity undertaken using a real tray and physical objects. Learners may also have, or be able to access, physical resources to support the learning they undertake in a virtual classroom. For example, dental technicians studying at Cardiff Metropolitan University attend weekly virtual classroom sessions for tutor input and discussion of practical tasks (Lewis, personal communication, 2013). These tasks are then carried out in laboratory facilities that are close to the student's location rather than on the university campus. Although this model relies in part on the goodwill of local employers to support student technicians, Parcell (2011) reports that the approach has increased the flexibility and accessibility of the course whilst at the same time reducing demands on university resources and travel costs for students and employers.

As well as drawing on learners' own physical resources, sophisticated online tools exist which support simulations and practical activities in many disciplines. These include online microscopes, virtual patients and virtual laboratories. Application sharing, web tours and file exchange functions in the virtual classroom may facilitate shared views or even collaborative exploration of some of these resources. Sharing of other offline experiences can also be facilitated with web conferencing. For example, students on a teacher training course were asked to make videos of their classroom practice for discussion in the virtual classroom. A tutor evaluates the experience.

> The videos prompted valuable discussions and revealed all manner of things that students hadn't previously thought about. One student noticed that pupils were easily distracted on their way to access materials in one area in his classroom and proposed some reorganisation. Another was surprised at how much information she could get from pupils' body language. Shared viewing using the virtual classroom was only possible where the student had a particularly good internet connection, and for those who didn't we compromised by watching the video independently and then coming together for a discussion online. However, capturing

stills from the video and displaying these on the whiteboard was still a great way to bring the student's class into the conversation and I would not hesitate to recommend this as an approach in the future.

A creative solution to technical problems created by varying bandwidth availability was needed in this case, and it may be that activities which require additional software, such as virtual worlds, are better integrated as part of a blended online strategy (see below) rather than trying to bring them directly into the virtual classroom. Any novel use of external resources requires preparation and practice, particularly if learners need to have additional equipment available.

Learners and experts

Outside experts are another resource which may be available to support learners. This tutor exploits the possibilities offered by web conferencing for bringing together learners and experts.

We engage practitioners from the community to work with our students. We have face to face visits from practitioners, but before they come to see us we use web conferencing sessions to send questions, or to do a preliminary 'what we would really like to know when you visit us' discussion. We also use web conferencing to keep in touch with them after their visits, so they don't actually have to be on the campus but they can continue to have an interest in the students that they've spoken to.

This is a sophisticated way to integrate external experts into a learning context, but there are much more straightforward approaches, including simply inviting them online to give a presentation or to answer learners' questions as part of a session. You may need to reassure yourself that your guest expert is comfortable in the virtual classroom and they may need an opportunity to practice before the live event. If the guest speaker is new to web conferencing, briefing them on approaches that work and advising them to avoid a lengthy presentation is helpful. The facilitator role during such events often switches to that of a moderator who offers support to the guest and encourages interaction between learners and expert. This guest expert experience illustrates good preparation.

> My guest slot was a very rewarding experience! I did have prior experience as a facilitator, and with the software that the course used, and that probably helped things run smoothly. The team running the course provided me with the session aims, details about participants, a precise time slot, what and why they would record and so on before I agreed to contribute. I provided copies of my slides in advance and we ran through them before the session – I was keen to do this having seen another guest presenter struggle when his carefully prepared presentation didn't display as expected in a different web conferencing environment. I think it important that a guest slot for a live online session includes some interaction otherwise you could just send a video recording. So I included questions for the audience and made sure that there was time for their questions too. It was a large group on the day and difficult to gauge who was in the audience – I couldn't even see all the names on the participant list at once. I started with a few questions to find out about them – their background, context, why they were interested and so on. They answered in the chat box and it was helpful to feel I was getting to know them a bit before I started.

This guest enjoyed the experience of contributing to a live online session, but there are many challenges for an expert who is not so familiar with the software or facilitating live online sessions, and your own guest speakers may need more support to ensure a successful experience for the guest as well as learners.

Local and remote learners

Web conferencing offers the opportunity to bring together local and distant learners. Projecting the virtual classroom at the front of the class and using a table top microphone opens up opportunities for group interaction with a single person or several learners at a distance. This approach can be used to bring an expert into a face to face class where the presenter is remote and the audience all together, but with a bit of creativity many variations can be tried. It could be one or more students who are at a distance from the rest of the class. Some preparation will be necessary to ensure that remote participants are comfortable with the software, and it is useful to have a local facilitator to support the class and operate the software. Ideally this should be someone who can diagnose any technical or audio problems and help ensure the software is used appropriately.

An approach that can be adapted from conference settings is to have the presenter in the room with part of the class and remote classmates online and contributing primarily through text or using audio when appropriate. This allows local and distance participants to come together to experience a learning opportunity. A variation on this approach is reported in Steele (2012). On an innovative pilot food hygiene course, remote work based learners used web conferencing to join classroom peers. Some issues had to be addressed to allow all learners' needs to be met. For example, separate induction arrangements were put in place for face to face and distance learners, and a video was suggested as a means to allow remote learners to experience the kitchen tour provided in the college. Audio problems were experienced, but remote learners were prepared to tolerate some technical difficulties. The project report suggests that the approach would be transferable to other settings if appropriate technical support and user connectivity were in place.

A more ambitious approach is to run a whole course this way, as was successfully achieved by a colleague who had one remote participant unable to travel to join class. After problems were experienced sharing resources whilst video conferencing with this student, web conferencing was used instead and allowed much more effective participation. Some additional facilitation strategies may be necessary to accommodate such a situation. The tutor reported that she needed to repeatedly check whether the remote student was appropriately engaged or wanted to add anything. She had to deliberately create opportunities and spaces for him to contribute to group activities, and found that booking two physical rooms allowed effective small group discussions which could include him but at the same time remain private. Moving the microphone around was important to provide good quality audio, and using video helped to provide a sense of social presence.

> We usually just scan the camera round and then leave it on a group shot. I've quite often just picked up the web cam and taken it round so that he can see the people that are there, and we make sure that everyone speaks so that he becomes familiar with the voices again. Everyone says this is really nice, you can see him in his kitchen and you can see when he's gone.

The student also found strategies to help him, such as using two computers so that he could have handouts and other documents available onscreen at the same time as the web conferencing interface. This had the added benefit of increasing the sense of contact and presence that might be lost if continual switching between windows was necessary.

Blending online approaches

Blending live online sessions with other online approaches, such as asynchronous discussions, wikis, blogs or virtual worlds, creates numerous innovative and creative learning opportunities. For instance, a course which consists largely of independent study of prerecorded lectures and other online resources can be given shape and structure through periodic synchronous sessions. Very large-scale online courses frequently build on this approach, offering resources for independent study, encouraging collaboration with peers for discussion and assessment, and providing opportunities for interaction with tutors through live online sessions. The live sessions may also be recorded to maintain the flexibility required when a course has a large number of participants.

Whilst a very large online course may have thousands of participants, on a course with a smaller group of learners a web conferencing session can be followed by a more structured asynchronous discussion activity in which learners demonstrate deeper engagement with course topics or the application of ideas to their own context. This can be very effective if learners prepare thoughtful postings and engage in meaningful interaction with each other. However, asynchronous discussions can be difficult to manage since they require a different set of facilitation skills to those needed for live online learning. In addition, they may not be the optimal method of communication when synchronous alternatives are available, as this learner experience suggests.

> During our course we had a virtual classroom session and were then given a set of questions to discuss further in the discussion forum of our VLE (Virtual Learning Environment). Personally, I would have preferred to continue the conversations in the virtual classroom. For me the discussion forum tool is not very exciting and it felt like you were posting answers and opinions into a black hole. There was some feedback from the tutors, but it wasn't really a discussion. Perhaps it's a personal thing, but I really don't like online discussion forums because they are often very unstructured and very abstract, and it's difficult to see a cohesive thread through them.

An interesting example of the integration of web conferencing with asynchronous discussions is an online role play activity run at La Trobe University in Australia (Keeffe and Austin, 2012). Web conferencing sessions were used to start and conclude a role play, with anonymous asynchronous discussions taking place in between. The initial live session allowed the tutor to ensure that learners fully understood the aims of the activity and their roles and responsibilities before they embarked on the role play itself. The closing session provided an opportunity for participants to reflect on their experiences and for the tutor to draw out key learning points. This model is adaptable to other contexts and illustrates the effective use of web conferencing to support something that could not be done face to face, since anonymous interactions would be impossible within a classroom setting.

These are just a few examples, but the possibilities for blending technologies are probably endless. For instance, a live online session could be used to plan collaborative work on a wiki, to review progress with reflective blogs, or for learners to discuss their experiences of social networking.

As well as extending the reach of web conferencing, other tools can be employed to overcome some of the limitations of current web conferencing tools. For example, in some current web conferencing systems PowerPoint annotations, animations and hyperlinks are lost if slides are imported to a whiteboard. Other systems allow upload of presentations created using some software packages but not others. All software has limitations and idiosyncrasies and creative solutions to technical limitations will always be necessary.

Exploring the potential of live online learning

Most facilitators quickly become comfortable and familiar with a particular range of web conferencing tools and re-use them regularly. They might stick predominantly with these well known tools, perhaps to save time, effort, or even embarrassment if something were to go wrong. The result can be predictable sessions which, after a while, may fail to engage learners or provide memorable learning experiences.

A lack of confidence may be one reason for not using software tools to their full potential. Another is a lack of inspiration or ideas about how to use the tools. As an example take the option to make recordings of live sessions. Recordings are usually easy to create and they are often provided to learners who unable to attend a session, but they can also be used in many other ways. They can:

- be edited to create different types of learning opportunities
- be made available in full or in part for revision activities

- help new students prepare for a live session
- provide potential students with an insight into the virtual classroom space
- be used for assessment purposes
- support self-evaluation by learners
- assist those with language or memory difficulties
- provide a valuable opportunity for the facilitator to review and reflect on practice.

There are probably other ways to use recordings, particularly when the possibilities of recording individual modes of communication (such as text chat) are taken into account. But how many have you seen being used in practice or tried out yourself? Even if you do use recordings regularly, are there new ways you could use the tools you are already familiar with?

We have attempted to cover many of the features and functions of web conferencing software in this book, but we have not tried to cover everything. As well as new ways to use the tools you already employ regularly, there are probably other tools to explore. Some may be particularly relevant to your own context, perhaps planning tools, functions for editing and sharing recordings of sessions, or those for developing and using quizzes. One way to find out what else is on offer is to consult the product manuals, handbooks and help systems but the next section considers the impact that collaboration with others can have on your practice and confidence with live online learning. It takes commitment and patience to keep challenging yourself to explore and appreciate the full range of functions that the software offers.

Collaborating for creativity

An alternative productive way to discover new tools and meaningful ways of using the software is through collaboration. Observing someone else facilitating live online learning or participating in a course as a learner may reveal alternative ways of using the tools available, or uncover some that have remained unexploited in your own practice. Another effective way to develop your practice is to work in partnership with another facilitator, since they can be a source of inspiration, encouragement and support as you try something new, as this tutor recognizes.

> I had not been brave enough to try the application sharing features of the software in a live session. I was concerned that there might be problems such as me inadvertently sharing my whole desktop or the contents of my

email system with students, so I avoided using it, even though I was aware of the advantages. When an overseas contact suggested we use web conferencing to work on a joint paper, the opportunity to share our document so that we could discuss it was too good to miss, and I had a go. I let him take the lead and do the sharing, and it worked pretty well. The experience also gave me an idea of what the experience would be like from the student perspective. This gave me the push I needed to try it with my students. It all went well and sharing documents and other files has now become a regular feature of my sessions – and I'm particularly pleased that I've even been able to do it on an impromptu basis when the need has arisen!

The tutor below also acknowledges the value of collaboration as a way of developing her own creativity and skills in using web conferencing, and the importance of standing back from facilitation to observe and reflect on what is possible.

Hanging around other people's sessions and team discussions are real prompts to creativity. That and listening to your learners and listening to the participant who isn't able to take part for some reason, trying to identify the barriers they face and work out responses. For me the development process is very much active learning, I need to be in an environment, to stumble over something and fail to do something before I really start to think about what the solutions are. If I'm there and I watch someone else solve a problem that can be such a tremendous moment. You think 'Ahh – they've done it, they know how to do it.' I've experienced that in all the shared sessions I've done, and I think it shows that somehow your own thinking is too busy and too preoccupied with the session you are running. When you are facilitating you don't pay attention to some of the process things that it would be really helpful to learn, because you're trying to pay attention to too many things at once.

Another experienced tutor identifies what she wants to do to exploit the full potential of live online learning. The focus here is not on expanding her repertoire of technical skills, but understanding the affordances or benefits that the technology offers so that these can be shared with learners.

What I want to be able to do is really unpick where synchronous online learning is valuable as a learning environment and a learning experience and get a greater understanding of how it enhances leaning and affords opportunities that are not possible elsewhere. I suppose it's a little bit about 'selling it'. If people are coming to us for our courses we need to justify why we are not doing it face to face and why we insist that our online learning experience still has this live component. Is it really just a cost saving thing? Is it really so that we don't have to travel? Surely it's more than that. Surely it's because there are experiences possible using these tools that develop learning and help learners develop their thinking in a way that's perhaps different from a face to face group.

Enhancing opportunities for learning and understanding the limits of the software may require dialogue with technical support staff and software vendors. Providing developers with feedback on the issues and problems faced across diverse learning situations helps them understand the needs of learners and facilitators. It enables them to develop their products appropriately to suit our contexts. There is an opportunity for teachers and trainers to influence the future direction of live online learning by engaging with this wider community, perhaps through vendor webinars, as part of institutional reviews or at conferences and software exhibitions. In turn, this will provide facilitators with a better understanding of the potential of the technology and the ways in which it can be used to support learning.

IN SUMMARY

Adopting a learner centred approach to live online learning means considering all of your learners' needs and characteristics to help you design and facilitate effective and engaging learning activities. The challenges associated with diverse learner groups can often be overcome using web conferencing in ways that would be impossible in a face to face classroom context. Some of the examples provided in this chapter illustrate creative approaches that address specific problems. This chapter has provided examples which show how:

- Accommodating the needs of an individual can often benefit a whole group of learners and **create an inclusive and accessible learning environment** for all learners. Cultural and language issues should be considered when working with international learners, and the specific requirements of those with physical impairments, justifiable media preferences and diverse previous experiences can be accommodated with careful design and preparation.

- **Creative applications of web conferencing** in different contexts can provide opportunities for learning not available in other ways, or approaches that overcome limitations and constraints of existing settings. Bringing together learners with resources, experts and other learners that they would not otherwise be able to engage with, and blending the use of live online learning with other online approaches can provide inspiring and engaging learning opportunities not otherwise possible.
- **Exploring the potential of web conferencing technology** requires an openness to new ideas, a willingness to explore the technology fully, and a commitment to take measured risks to test out new strategies and approaches. It can be supported effectively by working with others, using opportunities for collaboration to design and deliver live online learning or through discussion and observation of other facilitators' practice.
- **Good tutors and trainers are always learners themselves**. As a live online tutor or trainer you need to be open to new situations and opportunities for the use of live online learning, and ready to adapt your design approaches and facilitation strategies to enable you to meet the needs of all learners.

Continuing the journey

Exploring the full potential of web conferencing is clearly not just about technical proficiency, effective planning and preparation and flawless facilitation, although all of these aspects are important. Effective facilitation of live online learning should help learners become progressively more autonomous and able to take responsibility for their own learning. Web conferencing software creates new opportunities for teaching and learning which can support this aim. It allows activities and interactions that would be impractical or even impossible in other teaching and learning contexts. It can be used to create an inclusive environment in which all learners can be supported and encouraged to contribute. It provides a platform for distributed learners to work together as part of a supportive learning community.

Facilitation of live online learning with web conferencing is demanding and challenging, but also exciting and rewarding. It requires an understanding of learners, appropriate technical expertise, and a creative and flexible learner centred approach. It requires a curiosity about learners and learning, a desire to make learning effective, and a willingness to take risks and learn from your own experiences.

We have shared the examples, insights and strategies in this book to demonstrate how an empty virtual classroom can be transformed into an effective learning space and hope that this has inspired you to explore the full potential of web conferencing to support your own learners. Your travels into the virtual classroom may be just beginning, or they may have started some time ago, but we also hope that as part of the wider community of facilitators you have been encouraged to continue develop your own practice in live online learning and to share your successes and challenges to benefit all our learners.

Suggested further reading

Teaching, learning, assessment and reflective practice

Brookfield, S. (1995) *Becoming a critically reflective teacher.* San Francisco: Jossey Bass.

Chickering, A. and Gamson, Z. (1989) *7 principles for good practice in undergraduate education.* Racine, WI: Johnson Foundation.

Entwistle, N. J. (2009) *Teaching for understanding at university: deep approaches and distinctive ways of thinking.* Basingstoke: Palgrave Macmillan.

Hillier, Y. (2002) *Reflective teaching in further and adult education.* London: Continuum.

Hunt, L. and Chalmers, D., eds. (2012) *University teaching in focus: a learning-centred approach.* Abingdon: Routledge.

Moon, J. (1999) *Reflection in learning and professional development: theory and practice.* London: Kogan Page.

Rogers, A. and Horrocks, N. (2010) *Teaching Adults*, 4th edition. Maidenhead: Open University Press.

Sambell, K., McDowell, L. and Montgomery, C. (2013) *Assessment for learning.* Abingdon: Routledge.

Strategies and resources for tutors and trainers

Bligh, D. (2000) *What's the point in discussion?* Chicago: University of Chicago Press.

Boud, D. (1995) *Enhancing learning through self-assessment.* London: Kogan Page.

Brookfield, S. and Prenskill, S. (2005) *Discussion as a way of teaching: tools and techniques for democratic classrooms.* 2nd edition. San Francisco: Jossey Bass.

Carroll, J. and Ryan, J., eds. (2005) *Teaching international students: improving learning for all.* Abingdon: Routledge.

Jaques, D. and Salmon, G. (2007) *Learning in groups: a handbook for face to face and online environments.* Abindgon: Routledge.

Jones, K. (2002) *Icebreakers: sourcebook of games, exercises and simulations.* 2nd edition. London: Kogan Page.

Race, P. (2000) *500 tips on group learning.* London: Kogan Page.

Race, P. (2007) *Lecturers' Toolkit: a practical guide to assessment, learning and teaching.* 3rd edition. Abingdon: Routledge.

Svinicki, M. and McKeachie, W. J. (2011) *McKeachie's teaching tips: strategies, research and theory for college and university lecturers.* 13th edition. Wadsworth: Cengage Learning.

Online and technology-enhanced learning

Anderson, T., ed. (2008) *Theory and practice of online learning.* Canada: Athabasca Press. Available from: http://www.aupress.ca/index.php/books/120146 (accessed 3 November 2013).

Beetham, H., Sharpe, B. and De Freitas, S., eds. (2013) *Rethinking pedagogy for a digital age: designing for 21st century learning*. 2nd edition. Abingdon: Routledge.
Bonk, C. J. and Zhang, K. (2008) *Empowering online learning: 100+ activities for reading, reflecting, displaying and doing*. San Francisco: Jossey Bass.
Harasim, L. (2010) *Learning theory and online technologies*. Oxford: Routledge Falmer.
Herrington, J., Reeves, T. C., and Oliver, R. (2010) *A guide to authentic e-learning*. London: Taylor and Francis.
Ingle, S. and Duckworth, V. (2013) *Enhancing learning through technology in lifelong learning: fresh ideas, innovative strategies*. Maidenhead: Open University Press.
JISC (2009) *Effective practice in a digital age: a guide to technology-enhanced learning and teaching*. Bristol: JISC. Available from: http://www.jisc.ac.uk/whatwedo/programmes/elearningpedagogy/practice.aspx (accessed 3 November 2013).
Salmon, G. (2007) *E-moderating: the key to online teaching and learning*. 2nd edition. Abingdon: Taylor and Francis.
Salmon, G. (2013) *E-tivities: the key to active online learning*. 2nd edition. Abingdon: Taylor and Francis.
Seale, J. (2013) *e-learning and disability in higher education: accessibility research and practice*. Abingdon: Routledge.
Stefani, L., Mason, R. and Pegler, C. (2007) *The educational potential of e-portfolios: supporting personal development and reflective learning*. Abingdon: Routledge.

Live online learning with web conferencing

Chatterton, P. (2012) *Designing for participant engagement with Blackboard Collaborate*. Bristol: JISC. Available from http://www.jisc.ac.uk/whatwedo/programmes/elearning/collaborateguidance.aspx (accessed 3 November 2013).
Clark, R.C. and Kwinn, A. (2007) *The new virtual classroom: evidence based guidelines for synchronous e-learning*. San Francisco: Pfeiffer.
Cornelius, S. and Gordon, C. (2012) 'Learners' experiences of synchronous online activities: project report'. University of Aberdeen. Available from: www.slideshare.net/sarahcornelius (accessed 3 November 2013).
Finkelstein, J. (2006) *Learning in real time: synchronous teaching and learning online*. San Francisco: Jossey Bass.
Hoffman, J. (2003) *The synchronous trainer's survival guide*. San Francisco: Pfeiffer.
Hoffman, J. (2004) *Live and online: tips, techniques and ready to use activities for the virtual classroom*. San Francisco: Pfeiffer.
Shepherd, C. and Sampson, B. (2010) ALT/ELN webinar: How to run a virtual classroom session, 02 August 2010. Available from: http://repository.alt.ac.uk/803/ Association for Learning Technology (accessed 3 November 2013).
Shepherd, C., Green, P. and Sampson, B. (2011) *Live online learning: a facilitator's guide*. Chesterfield: Onlignment. Available from: http://onlignment.com/live-online-learning-a-facilitators-guide/ (accessed 3 November 2013).
Steed, C. (2011) *Facilitating live online learning*. Engaged Online Learning.

References

Anderson, T., ed. (2008) *Theory and practice of online learning.* Canada: Athabasca Press. Available from: http://www.aupress.ca/index.php/books/120146 (accessed 3 November 2013).

Beetham, H., Sharpe, B. and De Freitas, S., eds. (2013) *Rethinking pedagogy for a digital age: designing for 21st century learning.* 2nd edition. Abingdon: Routledge.

Bennett, P. W. (2012) *The sky has limits: online learning in Canadian K-12 public education. A report prepared for the Society for Quality Education.* Toronto, Ontario. Available from: http://www.societyforqualityeducation.org/parents/theskyhaslimits (accessed 3 November 2013).

Bligh, D. (2000) *What's the point in discussion?* Chicago: University of Chicago Press.

Bonk, C. J. and Zhang, K. (2008) *Empowering online learning: 100+ activities for reading, reflecting, displaying and doing.* San Francisco: Jossey Bass.

Boud, D. (1995) *Enhancing learning through self-assessment.* London: Kogan Page.

Bower, M. (2011) 'Synchronous collaboration competencies in web conferencing environments – their impact on the learning process'. *Distance Education*, 32(1), 63 83.

Brookfield, S. (1995) *Becoming a critically reflective teacher.* San Francisco: Jossey Bass.

Brookfield, S. (2006) *The Skillful Teacher.* San Francisco: Jossey Bass.

Brookfield, S. and Prenskill, S. (2005) *Discussion as a way of teaching: tools and techniques for democratic classrooms.* 2nd edition. San Francisco: Jossey Bass.

Brown, S. and Race, P. (2012) 'Using Effective Assessment to Promote Learning'. In Hunt, L. and Chalmers, D., eds, *University Teaching in Focus: a learning-centred approach.* Abingdon: Routledge. pp. 74–91.

Canning, R. (2008) 'Reflecting on the Reflective Practitioner: muddled thinking and poor educational practices'. Conference paper *UCET Conference*, 2008, Birmingham.

Carroll, J. (2005) 'Strategies for being more explicit'. Chapter 4 in Carroll, J. and Ryan, J. (eds.) *Teaching international students: improving learning for all.* Abingdon: Routledge.

Carroll, J. and Ryan, J., eds. (2005) *Teaching international students: improving learning for all.* Abingdon: Routledge.

Chatterton, P. (2012) *Designing for participant engagement with Blackboard Collaborate.* Bristol: JISC. Available from http://www.jisc.ac.uk/whatwedo/programmes/elearning/collaborateguidance.aspx (accessed 3 November 2013).

Chickering, A. and Gamson, Z. (1989*) 7 principles for good practice in undergraduate education.* Racine, WI: Johnson Foundation.

Clark, R.C. and Kwinn, A. (2007) *The new virtual classroom: evidence based guidelines for synchronous e-learning.* San Francisco: Pfeiffer.

Cornelius S (2013a) 'Convenience and community? An exploratory investigation into learners' experiences of web conferencing'. *Journal of Interactive Learning Research*, 24(3), 267–283.

Cornelius, S. (2013b) 'Facilitating in a demanding environment: experiences of teaching in virtual classrooms using web conferencing'. *British Journal of Educational Technology.* [Available from http://onlinelibrary.wiley.com/doi/10.1111/bjet.12016/abstract. DOI: 10.1111/bjet.12016].

Cornelius, S. and Gordon, C. (2012) 'Learners' experiences of synchronous online activities: project report'. University of Aberdeen. Available from: www.slideshare.net/sarahcornelius (accessed 3 November 2013).

Cornelius, S. and Gordon, C. (2013) 'Facilitating learning with web conferencing: recommendations based on learners' experiences'. *Education and Information Technology*, 18(2), 275–285.

De Freitas, S. and Neumann, T. (2009) 'Pedagogic strategies supporting the use of Synchronous Audiographic Conferencing: a review of the literature'. *British Journal of EducationalTechnology*, 40(6), 980–998.

Dochy, F., Segers, M. and Sluijsmans, D. (1999) 'The use of self-, peer and coassessment in higher education: A review'. *Studies in Higher Education*, 24(3), 331–350. Available from: http://www.tandfonline.com/doi/abs/10.1080/03075079912331379935#.UoT8DifU6PQ. DOI 10.1080/03075079912331379935.

Duemer, L., Fontenot, D., Gumfory, K., Kallus, M., Larsen, J., Schafer, S., and Shaw, B.C. (2002) 'The use of synchronous discussion groups to enhance community formation and professional identity development'. *The Journal of Interactive Online Learning*, 1(2), 1–12.

Entwistle, N. J. (2009) *Teaching for understanding at university: deep approaches and distinctive ways of thinking*. Basingstoke: Palgrave Macmillan.

Finkelstein, J. (2006) *Learning in real time: synchronous teaching and learning online*. San Francisco: Jossey Bass.

Garrison, D. R., Anderson, T. and Archer W. (2000) 'Critical enquiry in a text-based environment: computer conferencing in higher education'. *The Internet and Higher Education*, 2(2–3), 87–105.

Gordon C., Cornelius S. and Schyma J. 'Teaching with a blindfold on: best practice in Elluminate'. Conference proceedings 7th International Conference on Education, 7–9 July 2011, Samos, Greece.

Harasim, L. (2010) *Learning theory and online technologies*. Oxford: Routledge Falmer.

Herrington, J., Reeves, T. C., and Oliver, R. (2010) *A guide to authentic e-learning*. London: Taylor and Francis.

Hillier, Y. (2002) *Reflective teaching in further and adult education*. London: Continuum.

Hoffman, J. (2003) *The synchronous trainer's survival guide*. San Francisco: Pfeiffer.

Hoffman, J. (2004) *Live and online: tips, techniques and ready to use activities for the virtual classroom*. San Francisco: Pfeiffer.

Hrastinski, S. (2008) 'Asynchronous and synchronous e-learning'. *Educause Quarterly*, 4, 51–55.

Hunt, L. and Chalmers, D., eds. (2012) *University teaching in focus: a learning-centred approach*. Abingdon: Routledge.

Ingle, S. and Duckworth, V. (2013) *Enhancing learning through technology in lifelong learning: fresh ideas, innovative strategies*. Maidenhead: Open University Press.

Ingle, S. and Duckworth, V. (2013) *Enhancing learning through technology in lifelong learning: fresh ideas, innovative strategies*. Maidenhead: Open University Press.

Jaques, D. and Salmon, G. (2007) *Learning in groups: a handbook for face to face and online environments*. Abindgon: Routledge.

JISC (2009) *Effective practice in a digital age: a guide to technology-enhanced learning and teaching*. Bristol: JISC. Available from: http://www.jisc.ac.uk/whatwedo/programmes/elearningpedagogy/practice.aspx (accessed 3 November 2013).

JISC TechDis (2013) 'TechDis: Inclusion technology advice'. Available from: http://www.jisctechdis.ac.uk/techdis/home (accessed 3 November 2013).

Jones, K. (2002) *Icebreakers: sourcebook of games, exercises and simulations*. 2nd edition. London: Kogan Page.

Keeffe, M. and Austin, L. 'Reciprocity, the rascal of resolution: Collaborative problem solving in an online role play'. In *Proceedings of the 4th International Conference on Computer Supported Education*, 2012, Porto, Portugal. pp. 252–257.

Kleimola, R. and Leppisaari, I. 'ePresence – a Key to Success in Online Education and Tutoring?' In J Luca and E Weippl, eds, *Proceedings of World Conference on Educational Multimedia, Hypermedia and Telecommunications*, 2008, Vienna, Austria, Chesapeake VA: AACE pp. 3430–3439.

Lampe, C., Donghee, Y., Vitak, J., Ellison, N. B., and Wash, R. (2011) 'Student use of Facebook for organizing collaborative classroom activities'. *International Journal of Computer Supported Collaborative Learning*, 6(3), 329–347.

Laurillard, D. (2002) *Rethinking university teaching: a conversational framework for the effective use of learning technologies*. 2nd edition. London: Routledge Falmer.

Lepsinger, R. and Lucia, A. (2009) *The Art and Science of 360 Degree Feedback*. Chichester: Wiley.

McBrien, J. L. and Jones, P. (2009) 'Virtual Spaces: employing a synchronous online classroom to facilitate student engagement in online learning'. *International Review of Research in Open and Distance Learning*, 10(3), 1–17.

Moon, J. (1999) *Reflection in learning and professional development: theory and practice*. London: Kogan Page.

Murphy, E., Rodríguez-Manzanares, M.A. and Barbour, M. (2010) 'Asynchronous and synchronous online teaching: Perspectives of Canadian high school distance education teachers'. *British Journal of EducationalTechnology*, 42(4), 583–591.

Offir, B., Lev, Y. and Bezalel, R. (2008) 'Surface and deep learning processes in distance education: synchronous versus asynchronous systems'. *Computers and Education*, 51(3), 1172–1183.

Parcell, L. (2011) 'Gathering and presenting evidence for sustainability of projects'. Blog posting. Available from: http://blog.rsc-wales.ac.uk/2011/01/17/gathering-and-presenting-evidence-for-impact-and-sustainability-of-projects/ (accessed 3 November 2013).

Race, P. (2000) *500 tips on group learning*. London: Kogan Page.

Race, P. (2007) *Lecturers' Toolkit: a practical guide to assessment, learning and teaching*. 3rd edition. Abingdon: Routledge.

Rogers, A. (2002) *Teaching Adults*. 3rd edition. Maidenhead: Open University Press.

Rogers, A. and Horrocks, N. (2010) *Teaching Adults*. 4th edition. Maidenhead: Open University Press.

Salmon, G. (2007) *E-moderating: the key to online teaching and learning*. 2nd edition. Abingdon: Taylor and Francis.

Salmon, G. (2011) *e-Moderating: the key to teaching and learning online*. 3rd Edition. Oxford: Routledge.

Salmon, G. (2013) *E-tivities: the key to active online learning*. 2nd edition. Abingdon: Taylor and Francis.

Sambell, K., McDowell, L. and Montgomery, C. (2013) *Assessment for learning*. Abingdon: Routledge.

Schön, D. A. (1987) *Educating the reflective practitioner*. San Francisco: Jossey-Bass.

Seale, J. (2013) *e-learning and disability in higher education: accessibility research and practice*. Abingdon: Routledge.

Shepherd, C. and Sampson, B. (2010) 'ALT/ELN webinar: How to run a virtual classroom session, 02 August 2010'. Available from: http://repository.alt.ac.uk/803/ Association for Learning Technology (accessed 3 November 2013).

Shepherd, C., Green, P. and Sampson, B. (2011) *Live online learning: a facilitator's guide*. Chesterfield: Onlignment. Available from: http://onlignment.com/live-online-learning-a-facilitators-guide/ (accessed 3 November 2013).

Shi, S. (2010) 'Teacher moderating and student engagement in synchronous computer conferences'. *MERLOT Journal of Online Learning and Teaching*, 6(2), 431–445.

Skylar, A. A. (2009) 'A comparison of asynchronous online text-based lectures and synchronous interactive web conferencing lectures'. *Issues in Teacher Education,* 18(2), 69–84.

Steed, C. (2011) *Facilitating live online learning*. Engaged Online Learning.

Steele, D. (2012) *SWEET project final report*. Bristol: JISC. Available from: http://www.jisc.ac.uk/whatwedo/programmes/elearning/swaniltig/sweet.aspx (accessed 3 November 2013).

Stefani, L., Mason, R. and Pegler, C. (2007) *The educational potential of e-portfolios: supporting personal development and reflective learning*. Abingdon: Routledge.

Svinicki, M. and McKeachie, W. J. (2011) *McKeachie's teaching tips: strategies, research and theory for college and university lecturers.* 13th edition. Wadsworth: Cengage Learning.

Valaitis, R., Noori Akhtar-Danesh, K.E., Levinson, A. and Wainman, B. (2007) 'Pragmatists, positive communicators and shy enthusiasts: Three viewpoints on web conferencing in health sciences education'. *Journal of Medical Internet Research* 9(5), e39.

Vitartas, P., Rowe, S. and Ellis, A. (2008) 'Students' first experiences with a Web conferencing system – preliminary findings'. *Proceedings of the Fourteenth Australasian World Wide Web conference, Australia 2008*. Available from: http://ausweb.scu.edu.au/aw08/papers/refereed/vitartas/paper.html (accessed 3 November 2013).

Wang, S-K. and Hsu, H-Y. (2008) 'Use of the webinar tool (Elluminate) to support training: the effects of webinar-learning implementation from student-trainers' perspective'. *Journal of Interactive Online Learning*, 7(3), 175–194.

Ward, M. E., Peters, G. and Shelley, K. (2010) 'Student and faculty perceptions of the quality of online learning experiences'. *International Review of Research in Open and Distance Learning*, 11(3), 57–77.

Index